An Olympian's Tryst with Soldiering

From Sansarpur to the Saragarhi Battalion (4 SIKH)

An Olympian's Tryst with Soldiering

From Sansarpur to the Saragarhi Battalion (4 SIKH)

Colonel Balbir Singh, VSM
Arjuna Awardee

THE BROWSER | FAUJI DAYS

Title: An Olympian's Tryst with Soldiering:
From Sansarpur to the Saragarhi Battalion (4 SIKH)
Author: Colonel Balbir Singh

ISBN: 978-93-92210-96-9

Published by:
JGS Enterprises Pvt Ltd
Imprint: The Browser

Publisher's Address:
SCO 14-15, FF, Sector 8-C, Chandigarh 160 009

Website: www.thebrowser.org
Email: service@thebrowser.in

Printed in India

© Layout and Cover Design by 99 beagles
www.99beagles.com

THE BROWSER
www.thebrowser.org
Publishers & Booksellers

FAUJI DAYS
www.faujidays.com
Oral History and Military Publishing

To
The individual and collective heritage in Sansarpur
and my mother, Darbar Kaur

1916-1979

Contents

The first Sikh to receive the Olympic Gold Medal, Col Gurmit Singh Kular scored seven goals with this hockey stick in the Los Angeles Olympics Games 1932. The magic hockey stick was manufactured by Uberoi Limited Sialkot in 1913 (now in Pakistan). My uncle's 112 years old precious gift is being preserved by me.

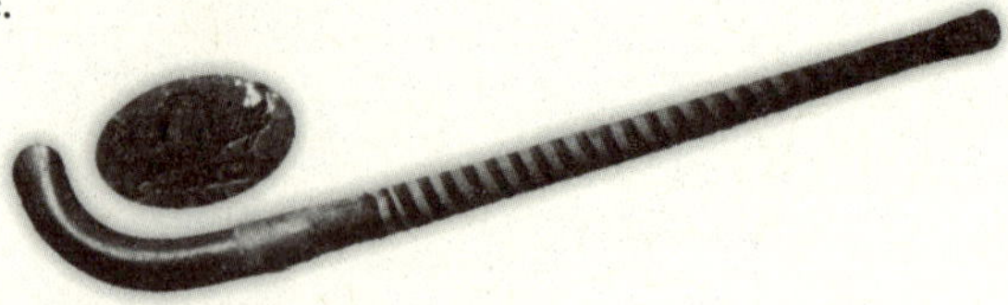

Lieutenant General PKG Menon, UYSM, AVSM receiving the final draft of Colonel Balbir Singh's new book—An Olympian's Tryst with Soldiering—an autobiographical account of the author as a soldier and a hockey player

Historically, hockey has been very popular with the Sikh Regiment. The keenness shown by the Colonel of the Regiment in thoroughly reading the contents was by no means a surprise to the author. During the interaction, he lauded the author's achievements and fondly remembered the 'golden era' of the Regiment team that produced so many Olympians. He acknowledged the contributions of Colonel Balbir Singh as a member of the Sikh Regiment team, a spirited soldier who was awarded the highest sports awards, the Arjuna Award, in 1968, making him the first Arjuna awardee in the Sikh Regiment.

The memoir subtitled *From Sansarpur to Saragarhi Battalion (4 SIKH)* is the quest of a die-hard regimental soldier and a sportsperson of international fame. The author inherited deep roots of camaraderie from his father, the late S Gajjan Singh, who served in 1 SIKH during the 1947 Indo-Pak war and was wounded while saving Srinagar from the rebels.

Sansarpur does not need any introduction as it has the global legacy of producing 14 Olympians and many more international players. The Saragarhi Battalion has a history associated with the soil of Sansarpur as it was raised in the adjoining Jalandhar Cantonment. The author coincidentally had the opportunity to play a tournament near the foothills of Saragarhi in Afghanistan in 1962 for the Indian University as a 16-year-old boy.

Deh Shiva Bar Mohey Ehai
Shubh Karman Te Kabhun Na Taron
Nah Daron Arison Jab Jaye Laron
Nische Kar Apni Jeet Karon

The Bully Off

Prologue

Destined Journey to The Rupa Valley

A strapping 20-year-old youngster travelled a long journey from Jalandhar to Missamari and thence by road to Rupa along the foothill route since there were hardly any roads and the terrain was mountainous and forested, to play for the 4 SIKH hockey team in the 11 Brigade Hockey Championship at Rupa Valley near Bomdila in North-East India, now Arunachal Pradesh, where the Battalion was then stationed. He changed three trains and took a steamer from Rangia as there was no bridge over the Brahmaputra to reach Missamari. Two Army men, Subedar DS Atwal and Havildar Piara Singh, accompanied the young man all the way from Jalandhar to Rupa at the behest of late Lieutenant Colonel Anant Singh, so great was the aura of this upcoming hockey player as he had already played in the 1964 Nationals for Punjab and exhibition matches against East Germany, Japan, and Malaysia.

Lieutenant Colonel Anant Singh, a great visionary, had already decided to induct him into the Army with a firm belief, awed as he was by the playing propensities of the young boy,

On the way to Rupa Valley (Lt Col Anant Singh, CO 4 SIKH, and Brig Prakash Singh Grewal, Commander 11 Brigade

confident that he would bring laurels to the nation and to the men in uniform. He was an extraordinary officer, ramrod in his physical appearance and, more importantly, in his dealings, official and personal.

Needless to state that the 11 Brigade championships was won and the young man, still not officially enrolled into the Army, was the highest scorer.

I was that young man who had reached Rupa Valley in an army vehicle driven by Lieutenant Colonel Anant Singh, the Commanding Officer, with Brigadier Prakash Singh Grewal, the Brigade Commander, sitting by his side. It was an honour to sit in the backseat of that Willys Jeep. Nothing could better exhibit the interest of senior army officers in sports in those days. My humble salutation to Lieutenant Colonel Anant

Singh, who was instrumental in inducting me to join 4 SIKH, formerly the 36th Sikh Saragarhi Battalion.

As Quoted by Col SS Duggal, 4 Sikh

After the Battle of Walong in 1962 against the Chinese, it required a herculean effort to get it (4 SIKH) back on a firm footing. The task of re-building the battalion into a well-knit team full of confidence and high morale was undertaken by Lieutenant Colonel Anant Singh, the commanding officer. Under his astute and dynamic leadership, 4 SIKH was a fully trained and operationally fighting fit unit capable of undertaking any task when it was launched in the 1965 war. His mettle was amply proved as he decided to capture a formidable objective like Barki without tank and artillery support and exhorted his men by saying, 'Each one of you is like a Centurion tank'. Mainly due to the Khemkaran debacle and no fault of the Commanding Officer, his valour went unrecognised. He was a leader with no parallel as a field commander and deserved the highest award. What a pity, Lieutenant Colonel Anant Singh, who got Barki, got nothing.

A Soldier Doesn't Die

Post the debacle of Khem Karan, Lieutenant Colonel Anant Singh wrote a letter to his daughter when he was sitting at the back in the jeep and being taken to Lakhpat Rai Jail, Lahore. He had a premonition that he wouldn't come back alive. He wanted Sukhi, being the eldest, to shoulder the responsibility of looking after the family in his absence. Hearing about this letter evoked an emotional response in me. The letter is reminiscent of the brave deeds of valiant soldiers.

A Soldier doesn't die when he fights for the nation,
but he dies when his nation forgets him.

On 18 December 2019, the Chief Minister of Punjab, Captain Amarinder Singh, honoured Sukhjinder Kaur, the daughter of Lieutenant Colonel Anant Singh, who commanded 4 SIKH during the operation in the 1965 War that led to the capture of Barki, which was one of the most decisive battles of the War.

Lieutenant Colonel Anant Singh's daughter, Sukhi, being honoured by the then Chief Minister Punjab, Captain Amarinder Singh

Lieutenant Colonel Anant Singh was taken to Lahore and media was called, seen smiling when JCO of Pak Army came and embraced him

On Receiving the Arjuna Award, the First in the Sikh Regiment, for the Year 1968

Lt Col ANANT SINGH
Assistant Director

[illegible]
17 Apr 69

My dear Balbir,

Please accept my heartiest congratulations on receiving the ARJUNA award for your superb performance in Hockey. You have been rightly called the best Half Line player in the Country and we are very proud of you.

2 Having brought you into the Services I naturally feel happy beyond limits. The Battalion too is proud of you.

3 Once again please accept my choicest felicitations.

With best wishes

Yours sincerely

DO written by Lieutenant Colonel Anant Singh on 17 April 1969

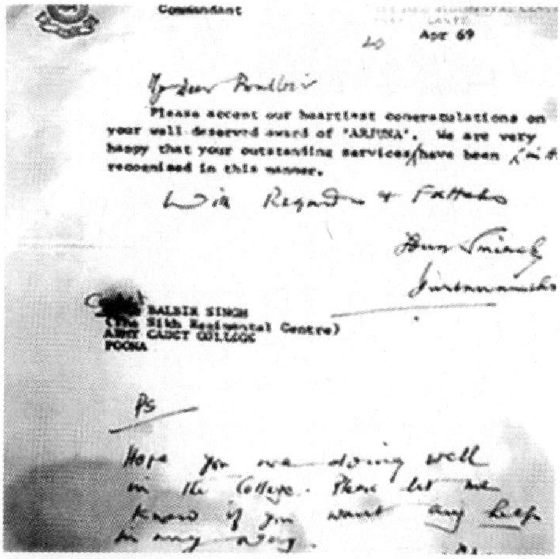

Commandant

20 Apr 69

My dear Balbir

Please accept our heartiest congratulations on your well deserved award of 'ARJUNA'. We are very happy that your outstanding services have been recognised in this manner.

With Regards & [illegible]

Cadet BALBIR SINGH
(The Sikh Regimental Centre)
ARMY CADET COLLEGE
POONA

PS

Hope you are doing well in the College. Please let me know if you want any help in any way.

DO written by Colonel Gurbaksh Singh, Commandant, Sikh Regimental Centre on 20 April 1969

Meeting Sub Darshan Singh Atwal years later

Back to the Past

Later in life, on 16 October 2019, I had the honour of meeting Subedar Darshan Singh Atwal again. Colonel SS Duggal and Subedar Modan Singh of 4 SIKH had apprised me that Subedar Darshan Singh Atwal was residing at Khurdpur near Adampur. He was 99 when I met him. He was the one who had taken me to Rupa Valley in 1964 to play hockey and join 4 SIKH as directed by Lieutenant Colonel Anant Singh, commanding officer of the battalion at that time. It was my great desire to meet him in person, as he was instrumental in shaping my destiny.

Darshan Singh Sahib, of course, did not recognise me as he could not have expected that I would one day pay a visit to him. He recalled very clearly and intelligently all the players of Sansarpur who were associated with 4 SIKH. I asked him if he remembered about Balbir. To my surprise, he narrated the journey from Jalandhar to Rupa Valley. His memory is still very sharp. He knew there was no enrolment in the Army, and a special sanction had been taken from Army HQ, Delhi, to enrol Balbir into 4 SIKH. He knew that Lieutenant Colonel Anant Singh had detailed officers of the rank of Captain to improve my essay writing skills.

It was a pleasant three-hour Interaction of reminiscences with him at his spacious house. I presented him with a woollen shawl (*loei*) as a gesture of goodwill.

He died on 5 February 2023 in his village, Khurdpur. I, unfortunately, could not attend his cremation as I was in Kolkata for our coursemates' get-together.

Sub Major Piara Singh

A Perfect Salute

I recall an amusing incident, etched in my mind, this was when I witnessed Sub Major Piara Singh of 4 SIKH on several occasions getting ready to give the first salute of the day to his 'CO Sahib'. The Sub Major who had a dynamic personality and good military bearing had a set drill before saluting his Commanding Officer. He would stand in attention in front of the Commanding Officer's tent and would wait at a fixed time and place. The Commanding Officer would also stand in attention in front of his tent and would wait for salutation from his Sub Major Piara Singh. After seeing his Commanding Officer in attention, he would take out his pocket mirror and set his mustaches and then would set his beard with the 'Baaz'. He would give a perfect salute to his Commanding Officer with a loud 'Sat Sri Akal'. It may be genuine, truly what it is said to be authentic to mention here that Sub Maj Piara Singh was the grandson of the SARAGARHI WAR HERO HAV ISHAR SINGH. A recent research was made by Mr Josan who visited the villages of most of the war heroes of Saragarhi to meet their descendants. He has depicted the photographs of these families on his website which shows the authenticity that they were married. Naik Bakhtor Singh who served with Sikh Regt is the fourth generation soldier of Hav Ishar Singh's family. This supersedes the under mentioned versions. The other version which differs is that 21 soldiers stationed at Saragarhi, were all bachelors, who had never married and so there are no direct descendents in India. They all offered their lives in the line of duty.

Yet another version is that out of 21 soldiers only Hav Ishar Singh was married but he did not have any issue and regarding his wife it is a mystery whether she had died or was eliminated/killed with an aim to grab the awarded money/land which was given to families of each of the fallen soldier. They were awarded Rs 500/- and two murabbas of land equivalent to 50 acres.

CHAPTER 1

4 Sikh, Saragarhi and Sansarpur

4 SIKH was originally raised as 36 SIKH in 1887 at Jullundur Cantonment very close proximity to Sansarpur where a large area was available thence. All basic training was

Major Charles Des Voeux (sitting, middle) with his men from the 36th Sikh Regiment Source: Captain Jay Singh-Sohal, British Library

given to the brave hearts on the soil of Sansarpur. After 10 years, the Saragarhi battle was fought in 1897. The path of the Saragarhi battalion's development in its infancy passed through the village of Sansarpur, areas wherein young soldiers were nurtured from 1887 to 1894, after which 36 SIKH moved to Manipur and then to Kohat on 20 December 1896.

In 1897, the Saragarhi piquet was held by 22 soldiers under the command of Havildar Ishar Singh, including Sep/Swr Daad. Braving all odds, the 22 braves of 36 SIKH fought to a bitter end. 21 of the soldiers were Jat Sikhs but with different surnames. The defenders of Saragarhi accounted for 450 Orakzai and Afridi-

Historical photograph of 5/13 Frontier Force hockey team, winners of the P.N.A.H.T Kohat district P.F.F, Radhu and Native Hockey Tournaments, 1934. My father Gajjan Singh is sitting on the right extreme. Lt Col R G Ekin sitting in the centre. Five players from Sansarpur were the members of the team. 21 soldiers of 36 SIKH had fought for Saragarhi in Kohat District in 1897.

Lashkar enemies killed before making the supreme sacrifice. Each Saragarhi hero was awarded an Indian Order of Merit, which was the highest gallantry award given to an Indian soldier in the British Army for valour and sacrifice. 21 IOMs, being awarded in one day for one battle had never happened before and has never happened since---they did the Regiment proud, and the British Parliament gave a standing ovation to honour the valour and sacrifice of Saragarhi Braves. The Battalion is known as the Janghi Paltan, and the combat ratio of defender vs. attacker was 1 to 500. Its motto is *'Nischay Kar Apni Jeet Karo'*, which applies to situations in life as well—if one decides to pursue a mission with resolve, then victory is inevitable.

It gives me goosebumps every time I read about the great Saragarhi battle; though I have not fought the battle in those rugged tribal areas of the North-West Frontier, I can imagine the tough conditions faced by the 22 soldiers of 36 SIKH during the battle.

I had the opportunity to see the Saragarhi Fort from a distance during my visit to Kabul, Afghanistan, for the Jashan Celebration Hockey Tournament in 1962 as a member of the Indian University Hockey team. The team travelled by rail through Pakistan, reached Peshawar by Frontier Mail and then by road to Kabul through Khyber Pass, Durand Line and the famous Jamrud Fort; it was amazing our bus wheezed its way over the Khyber Pass, neatly taking advantage of the deep valley slicing through the forbidden Hindu Kush Mountain range. The Khyber Pass is one of those geographical entities that has a near-mythical quality. The Pass has been the route of choice for an endless succession of invading armies down the centuries marching in from the rugged northwest.

There is no parallel to the bravery displayed by the 22 soldiers of 36 SIKH on 12 September 1897, yet it may not be possible to find a place on earth that can boast of having more Olympians and gold medallists than the Kulars of Village Sansarpur.

Sansarpur was more than a mere action of organising hockey in a systematic way. It is, in truth, a family, with its ancestors and descendants, its pride and its possessions, and through its vicissitudes, the ups and downs and changes in our life, a strong sense of community. This clearly reflects the enormous social prestige attached to hockey in Sansarpur, as detailed in the subsequent chapter.

Sansarpur Hockey Team, 1940

Standing: *Kehar Singh, Naranjan Singh, Sadhu Singh, Ajit Singh (4 SIKH), Nahar Singh, Ram Chand* ***Sitting:*** *Gulzar Singh, Captain Gurbachan Singh (Punjab Regiment), Captain Maluk Singh SB, OBI, IOM, Tara Singh, Mohan Singh (SIKH Regiment)* ***Ground:*** *Avtar Singh, Rajinder Singh*

First Army Hockey Tournaments: Delhi Darbar 1910–1911

The first Army Hockey Tournament was organised at Delhi Darbar in 1910–1911. 36 SIKH and 33 PUNJAB played in the finals, and 36 SIKH was the runners-up. The drum major, Sepoy Ishar Singh Kular, played as a left winger and was declared the best player in the tournament. (Quoted by my late father, Subedar Gajjan Singh of 1 SIKH.)

The Sikh Regimental Centre Hockey Team won the Nehru Gold Cup only once in the year 1965, and 4 SIKH players made a major contribution to winning the Cup. Five players from the battalion played the final match against Bombay XI on 5 November 1965 at Lady Harding Ground, New Delhi. Havildar Modan Singh (my real *bhua's* son) of 4 SIKH scored the only goal of the final. I feel proud that four Sansarpur players helped in winning the Nehru Cup.

The plethora of hockey players from Sansarpur who have represented 36 SIKH, now 4 SIKH are:

(a)	Sep Ishar Singh Kular (Drum Major, Delhi Durbar, 36 SIKH	1910-11
(b)	Sep Teja Singh Kular, 36 SIKH	1935-38
(c)	Sep Gurpal Singh Kular, 36 SIKH	Died in WW II
(d)	Sub Kapoor Singh Kular	1947-60
(e)	Sep Bikar Singh Kular	1947
(f)	Hav Ajit Singh Kular	Services team 1951
(g)	Sub Modan Singh Sohal	Services team 1966-67
(h)	Hony Lt Jaswinder Singh Kular	Services team 1966-68
(i)	Nk Gurdip Singh Kular	1964-1970
(j)	Sep Swaran Singh Kular	1964-1968
(k)	Balbir Singh Kular	Dec. 64 to Dec. 70

47 SIKH, now 5 SIKH, was part of the Jullundhur Brigade stationed in Jullundhur, close to Sansarpur. The Brigade moved to North Africa during the Second World War. The first-ever organised hockey match was played between 47 SIKH and The Manchester Guardian Regiment on Sansarpur land in 1910. It was a historical match with proper marking of the field and controlled by two umpires according to the rules of hockey at that time.

47 SIKH Hockey Team

Olympiam Gurmit Singh Kular of Sansarpur sitting second from right, and Captain (later Lt Gen) Harbaksh Singh sitting second from the left. Another player from Sansarpur sitting first from right.

Naik Naginder Singh Kular, the key player of the team as center-half died in WWII as he was hit by a gunshot in the chest. Before dying in front of his village-mate Captain Gurmit Singh Kular, he asked him to tell the village that he got a bullet in the front and not on the back. His younger brother, Gurpal Singh Kular of 36 SIKH (later 4 SIKH) also died in WWII.

CHAPTER 2

A Boy from Sansarpur

In my village, the lexicon predominantly consisted of two words, 'Hockey' and 'Soldiering'. And you will soon get to know me as a soldier and as 'Beera', the hockey player, but before I was either, I was just a simple outspoken boy from Sansarpur.

If the maxim is true, that children eventually become like their mothers, then all I can say is—I am very fortunate. My father was away fighting in the Second World War on December 8, 1944, the day I was born (as per my *janam patri*). I was the fourth child in my family and was named Balbir because it happened to be a very popular name in those days. I have four siblings, two sisters and two brothers.

An inspiration, a role model, a necessity for identity, a purpose for living; there can be myriad reasons behind the success of a sportsman. For me, it was the milieu I grew up in that developed my passion for hockey. The famous artist Andy Warhol once remarked that when he travelled across

America in the 1960s, he discovered that 'pop was everywhere', a reference to the youth culture and music that swept the West in that era. Anybody who travelled to Sansarpur in our time and after would have made the same discovery that hockey was everywhere. In fact, the joke was that if you threw a stone in Sansarpur, you would hit a hockey player!

The place where you are born often decides what you become. I was born in a humble family which did not have too many material possessions but valued what it had and did a lot of hard work to create it. I was to choose between a job with the Punjab Police and one with the Indian Army. In his spare but dramatic style, my father, an army man, told me to take a pen and a piece of paper and spell two words: A-R-M-Y and P-L-A-Y. When I wrote down those words, I now realise I had written down my own destiny, a feat that had become a habit with scores of international players from one narrow street in a village in Punjab. By army, my father meant hard work and determination; by play, he meant to focus on hockey and nothing else. Now, I can see that this one-track determination could have taken root only in a humble family like mine, where there was little to distract one from one's ambition and much to egg one forward.

From my early days to the end of my hockey-playing career, my family members have been my greatest source of inspiration. For me, it was easy to be in the game; my whole family was a great lover of hockey. I still fondly remember the day when my name was included for the first time in the list of Indian probables, and my father, Gajjan Singh Kular sent me a money order of Rs 200. In 1965, that was an inconsiderable sum of money. Moreover, the village elders were always there to encourage kids especially me to take up the game. The other influences that had their share in shaping the future of an impressionable young lad are innumerable.

I can vividly recall the day I played my first hockey tournament. It was in 1950, and the game was played on the hard surface of Sansarpur, Jullundur (as it was then spelt) Cantonment. It was organised by one-eyed bachelor Tara Singh Kular and featured teams from all the neighbouring villages. Tara lived in a small room near the Sansarpur hockey ground (we used to term it as '*Kane Tare di Attari*'). He used to take a keen interest in hockey, besides selling hockey sticks to Army units stationed at the Jullundur Cantonment. It was an emotional moment for me when my father, who used to be a hockey player, too, took me to Tara's room to select my first hockey stick. That small stick cost him all of two rupees small fortune in those distant days.

I played as centre half for the Sansarpur hockey team against Mithapur village in the final and was supported by Ajitpal, the full-back who later won India's 1975 World Cup. Tarsem Singh played in the forward line as a left winger, while Kulwant Singh of Mithapur played for his village. This handsome son of a schoolteacher now resides in Italy. Later, he represented India at the Munich Olympic Games in 1972. As long as 'Tara Singh' remained physically fit, he motivated the kids to participate in tournaments under various categories. This was a noteworthy contribution to the development of hockey and to Sansarpur in particular. To make it more entertaining, he started the custom of an entry fee for these weekend matches. Each player was supposed to shell out one anna (there were 16 annas to a rupee) each. The team that won the match got two annas as an incentive. Every player had to put in extra effort to best the opposing team. Old tennis balls were a common substitute for leather hockey balls, but there were no complaints. After all, it was the spirit of competing with other hockey players that we valued the most!

In summer, we looked forward to his famous annual 'Mango Party' of Safeda *aam*, specially organised for the young kids of Sansarpur under the big banyan tree that still stands near Olympian Jagjit's house. Like an IPL party of today's era (minus glitch and glamour), this was an annual get-together for all young hockey players...

I pursued my matriculation from Cantonment Board High School in the year 1960, Immediately after passing that, I was approached by none other than Prof. P.D. Choudhary (in charge of DAV College Jullundur's hockey team). He offered me free education, hostel facilities, and even Rs 30 for the tuck shop, along with a free bus travel pass from Jullundur Cantonment to DAV College. I accepted the grand offer with the aim of representing the university in hockey. In fact, Balbir Singh of Punjab Police, a Sansarpuri and fellow Olympian-to-be, was also a member of the same team. Our team reached the semi-finals in the Punjab University inter-college competition. The match was played on the Panjab University hockey ground at Chandigarh against Lyallpur Khalsa College, Jullundur, a well-fought match in which we lost by one goal. But as luck would have it, the upshot of it was that I was selected to represent the Panjab University team in the Inter-University Tournament (North Zone) at Aligarh. My immediate goal was fulfilled, and I felt as if I had arrived in my village.

Punjab University cleared the first hurdle, a difficult one, beating Delhi University in the semi-final and went on to beat the vaunted Aligarh Muslim University team. From Aligarh, we moved to Patna to play against Ranchi University, the East Zone winners. The match was played on the Gandhi Ground in Patna, and we happened to win by one goal to nil. The Patna crowd was aggressive and abusive. Just minutes before the final whistle, they decided to disrupt the match. As they charged in from the left flank of the ground, sensing trouble and to save ourselves, we hurriedly ran towards our changing room. Amidst this chaos, our left flank player from our village- Kuldip Singh, was captured by the aggressive Patna crowd. Locked in the dressing room, now, all we could hear were his screams, '*Oye marchadeya oye mar gaye. Bacho menu* (pleading us to rescue him) ...'. This rampage continued for 15 minutes. Even now, in our village, this episode is narrated to the entire village with laughter. Kuldip Singh, who lived in Calgary, Canada, died more than ten years back.

From there, we moved to Madras (now Chennai) and then to Annamalai University to play the final against Madras University. We won the championship! We played the final match at Annamalai University, which we won after a gap of seven years. The laurels went to Balbir Singh Kular (Captain and inside left), Balbir Singh Kular (right in), Jagjit Singh Kular (right half), Kuldip Singh Kular (left out), Mohinder Singh Kular (left half), Jasraj Singh Kular (forward) and Balbir Singh Kular (half back). (Spot me if you can!) As a reserve in that team, I lugged the three-foot huge trophy with a heavy wooden base to Punjab after four days of train travel.

Later, realising I was on a roll, I joined the famous Sports College at Jullundur in 1962. This institution was an initiative of the late Pratap Singh Kairon, the former Chief Minister of Punjab (he was tragically assassinated, shot dead in his car on the outskirts of Delhi), a keen sportsman in his younger days. As a member of the college team, I played in the 'B' Division of Punjab University. The Sports College won the championship in the very first year of its inception. I had finished my 12th, and it felt like my path in life was already being set in stone. Before I further move on to my story, it must be understood that my story is intertwined with the story of Hockey and Sansarpur. To untangle these threads would wilt the very core of who I am as a person. It would be fair to say then that my story started way before I was born.

How it Started: Hockey and Army

The British Army built Jullundur Cantonment in the proximity of the village in 1848, and seven barracks were built. The centre-most barrack was the largest and, distinguished by its weathercock, was predictably conferred the sobriquet of the *'Murghe Wali Barrack'* (The Barrack of the Cock) by the village folk. Between these barracks and Sansarpur village, there is a large field 500 yards square in area where, initially, British troops began playing hockey. Seeing them play, the Sansarpur people were also keen to try their hand at the game. The desire to rise from the orbit of middle-class status to stardom was figured by seeing smartly turned-out British officers and stories of their well-being through village elders.

Technically, the cantonment area was off-limits for civilians, but the British needed manpower for attending to minor chores, so no one objected when a few villagers were allowed into the area. Ground keeping being one such menial chore, it was quite logical to give the task to some villagers, who all came from agricultural stock and were familiar with the nuances of ground maintenance. Two of the earliest native groundsmen in the cantonment were Gama and Viri Deen. It was their job to water the field, chalk-mark the lines and take care of the general upkeep of the ground. Since such a heavy responsibility cannot be discharged efficiently by only two men, this resourceful pair induced some village children into helping them with their work. This led to further interaction between villagers and army men, with the two becoming integrated to the extent that the latter would allow villagers to play with them.

The army men further helped the village folk by giving them hockey sticks and balls that had been discarded by the army players (the villagers could not then afford to buy such fine equipment). Incidentally, the two Muslims, Gama and Viri (formerly Vir Deen), later became members of the Sansarpur hockey team in 1936 for the Beighton Cup when it was in its prime. The game of hockey, like any field sport, could only take root in areas where facilities are available, the most important of them being the availability of a playing ground: the actual equipment, in those days, was not very expensive. Villages close to Sansarpur and Cantonment, which therefore had access to the grounds, did imbibe the benefits of exposure to hockey played by the British and went on to make significant contributions to the game.

My Grandfather—Jagat Singh Kular

Sansarpur is representative of a culture steeped in folklore, very much a living entity. It all began centuries ago, when two real brothers, Baba Gursa Kular and Baba Bhagtu Kular, along with their nephew Baba Dhyan Singh Kular and two cousins, migrated from a village, Husanabad, situated near Srinh Shankar in the Nakodar tehsil, and settled at a place which later became known as Sansarpur. Of these five, only Baba Dhyan Singh Kular was initiated into Sikhism in the year 1699, when the mighty 10th Guru Gobind Singh formed the Khalsa. The area being unclaimed, these hardy pioneers proceeded to occupy land on all sides of the village and commenced agricultural operations. Perhaps the shift was to avoid the floods that plagued the former low-lying regions. It was one of the first homesteading initiatives in that region, but what's even more relevant now is the fact that Sansarpur is considered hallowed ground by ardent devotees of hockey, our national game.

Jagat Singh, son of Fateh Singh, was a descendant of Gursa. Jagat enrolled in the Army during British times. He joined the 35 SIKH and fought in the First World War for British India while on the strength of 35 SIKH, later called the Sikh

My grandfather on the left

Regiment Centre. He married Kishan Kaur of the Deol family, of village Khojewal near Kapurthala, and had two children, a son named Gajjan Singh (my father) and a daughter, Chanan Kaur. He put Gajjan in King George's School, Jalandhar, one of the best schools in North India those days. The school was inaugurated by no less a personage than the Prince of Wales in 1922. Besides his son, Jagat also brought up his nephew Teja Singh Deol of Khojewal village.

Teja was educated at ND Victor High School, Jalandhar Cantonment, from where he did his matriculation. Captain Teja Singh, who died at the ripe old age of 98, used to say that it was solely due to Jagat's benevolence in bringing him up at Sansarpur that he learnt hockey and enrolled in the Army, A British Captain from 2/12 Frontier Force came all the way from Sialkot by jeep to recruit young hockey players from Sansarpur, Teja was selected and taken to Sialkot. He always spoke highly of Jagat and gave him all the credit for moulding his life. In time, Jagat brought his daughter's son. Modan Singh to Sansarpur to ensure he received a good education. Modan, too, learnt the rudiments of hockey on the hard surface of Sansarpur. General Harbaksh Singh of the Sikh Regimental Centre sent a recruiting team headed by a Major (later Brigadier) Shamsher Singh Minhas to Sansarpur in 1960 to enrol hockey players. Modan made the cut and was enrolled in the 4 Sikh Regiment, along with others. He, too, gives full credit to his grandfather for reaching the national level in hockey. Modan retired as

Subedar. He enjoys the distinction of scoring the winning goal for SRC in the Nehru hockey final in 1965. The Sikh never won the Nehru hockey title after that. Jagat's benevolence and generosity are evident from the fact that he donated two plots of land measuring 1000 sq. yards to the Sansarpur Gurudwara and another to a backward class servant when his son Gajjan Singh was born.

I became the President of the Sansarpur Hockey Association after the death of the Olympian Udham Singh in 2000. Since then, it has been my earnest desire to get an astroturf laid in the village for the benefit of the new crop of budding players. My endeavours paid off when Sansarpur finally got a six-a-side synthetic hockey pitch laid in 2010 at the place where my grandfather had donated two of the nine kanals (a kanal is a plot of land roughly equal to 505.857 square meters or one-eighth of an acre) since donated to the village panchayat. Jagat never failed to attend weddings, especially those of the backward classes, even if uninvited, and would always make a *shagun* gift of one rupee, which was considered a substantial amount in those far-off days when money had value. Jagat and his wife stayed in a haveli, which was a sort of sprawling hacienda. The old couple were particular about their diet. My grandmother would grind fresh flour every day, never in her life did she fall ill, and medicines were unknown to her system. Jagat was very orderly, disciplined, and meticulous. As soon as he would come back from his army duty, he would change into field clothes and run to the fields to fetch fodder for his buffaloes. One of the many lessons that I learnt from my grandfather's example was hard work. I helped him in the fields, cutting hay, lifting, and stacking the heavy bundles of fodder. The hard physical labour gave me strength and stamina, and besides helping to shape my body, these assets later served me well in my athletic endeavours.

There were two jamun (Indian blackberry) fruit trees and a mango tree in the compound of the haveli where Jagat lived. Young boys, including later Olympians Tarsem and Ajitpal Singh, would come with a swarm of other boys to steal the fruit in the afternoon when my grandfather would be enjoying his siesta. To teach them a lesson, my grandfather collected some pebbles and hid them nearby. The next time the boys came to steal fruit, they got a rude shock; stones rained down on them when they climbed onto the Jamun trees. The boys fled helter-skelter and thereafter kept a respectable distance from the haveli.

Water for both people and cattle alike came from two small wells which had been dug in the village. Dr Jaswant Singh, father of Olympian Gurmit Singh (Olympics, 1932), constructed one well near the gurudwara, while my grandfather had the other dug within his haveli compound for the same purpose. Water had to be drawn from the well by hand, as they were not motorised. Sometimes, the village children would play a prank on grandfather by removing the ratchet that controlled the reverse turn of the handle. This caused the small iron water buckets to crash back into the well if one loosened one's grip on the handle for even a second. This was one trick that would make my grandfather hopping mad. Once, he gave a sound drubbing to a few boys (including my elder brother) for playing this prank just once too often.

My younger brother and I used to take his morning and evening tea to the haveli, where grandfather waited impatiently. In winter, the tea would get cold by the time it reached grandfather's hands, so my mother started putting glowing hot coals in an iron bucket, over which she kept the tea kettle so that it would reach grandfather in piping hot condition. We had no thermos flask in those days, but my mother's improvisation was such a grand success that a flask would have been entirely superfluous.

My grandfather was admitted twice to the Military Hospital at Jalandhar Cantonment. Once, he was so badly gored by his own cow that his stomach was ripped open. Unperturbed, he tucked his intestines back into the cavity, bandaged his stomach tightly with his turban and told his servant to take him to the Military Hospital. A month later, he was fit as a fiddle! Another time, he was sleeping outside in the open when a violent storm broke out. A branch from the Sheesham tree under which he was sleeping snapped in the gale-force winds and fell on his legs, fracturing them. He overcame this misfortune with a stoic heart. He seemed indestructible till he had a paralytic stroke. That slowed him down a lot. We brought him home from the haveli, and father nursed and attended him round the clock. But my grandfather was not one to be long dependent on others. He decided he had outlived his usefulness and chose to pass away peacefully one quiet afternoon in the spring of 1967.

My father—Gajjan Singh Kular

My father was educated in an English medium school and even stayed in the hostel. This was pretty rare in the India of the 1920s. After graduating, he joined 5/13 Frontier Force along with other hockey players from Sansarpur. One of the best hockey teams in the 30s, it won the Native Hockey Championships twice, even beating Dhyan Chand's Punjab Regiment in the finals, as my father was away on service a lot, it was left to my mother to manage the home front. This she did with remarkable

My Father
S. Gajjan Singh Kular

dedication. She made sure her brood of five children got an education, enforced strict discipline and inculcated good values in us.

Being a keen hockey player himself, my father's heart was set on my playing for India someday. He would frequently give me tips on how to improve my game, always fanning my interest in the game's subtleties in whatever way he could. Mother played her role well by concealing her fear (common to all mothers) that I would suffer some serious injury on the field. It was my father who guided me to play in both offensive as well as defensive modes. I followed his advice right up to my last match, scoring goals whenever I could while at the same time rushing back to cover the goalkeeper.

My father fought in the Second World War in West Asia while on the rolls of the 5/13 Frontier Force. After Partition, he joined the First Sikh Regiment. Whenever a new batch of officers joined the battalion, the Commanding Officer would give my father the job of training the newly commissioned officers. Colonel Harpal Kaushik, a member of the 1956, 1960 and 1964 Indian Olympic teams, and General BS Randhawa had high regard for my father for having groomed and nurtured them into officer material.

After he retired, my father settled in Sansarpur and followed the same routine as he had done in his childhood. He would go for a brisk morning walk, and in the evening, he would watch the kids playing hockey in the playground of Sansarpur, He led an orderly and disciplined life, having his meals at fixed times, taking care of all his routine maintenance needs, and reading the English newspapers thoroughly from cover. This accounted for his in-depth knowledge of current affairs.

After my mother's death on April 23, 1979, he continued staying at Sansarpur, with only a servant to care for his needs.

He refused to stay with any of his three sons, who would visit him occasionally to have a peg of rum. He led an independent life. He had adopted an orphaned lad from Jharkhand and brought him up. His devoted manservant stayed with him till his end. In his will, my father gifted his faithful Man Friday a small piece of land with a two-room cottage. The erstwhile boy still lives there, now a landed man of substance. For the last 25 years of his life, till he passed away, my father's routine was fixed. Every year, in the month of November, he would go to Delhi by the army bus along with the Army Service Corps hockey team to play in the Nehru Hockey Tournament. There, my father would stay with his eldest daughter for 15 days, watch all the matches and come back to Sansarpur with the hockey team.

In the year 1997, he was going with the Army XI hockey team on the bus when he had a heart attack near Panipat. Honorary Captain Gurdev Singh from SRC, an international player, and KP Singh from ASC, who was also a Services hockey coach, immediately administered first-aid to him before taking him to a local doctor. On the latter's advice, they shifted him to RR Hospital in Delhi Cantonment. He recovered soon after. I went to Delhi to bring my father back to Jalandhar, and Pritam Singh, his son-in-law, took him to the RR Hospital for what turned out to be his last check-up. He had a massive attack in the lift and collapsed in front of his son-in-law. He died on December 27, 1997. My brother-in-law Pritam, my sister and I made arrangements for my father's body to be transported to Sansarpur for the cremation. Many well-known Olympians attended his last rites. Ironically, the late Olympian Udham Singh, my father's best friend, was deeply moved by this tragic loss.

The Tribune – 31st Dec '97

BHOG & ANTIM ARDAS

With profound grief and sorrow we inform the sad demise of our father **S. GAJJAN SINGH s/o S. Jagat Singh.**

Bhog Sri Akhand Path, Kirtan and Antim Ardas for the peace of departed soul will be held on **31 Dec. 97, Wednesday between 12 Noon to 1 p.m. at Gurdwara Village Sansarpur, Jalandhar Cantt.** (Guru ka Langar 1 p.m.)

Prof Pritam Singh Bains — Mandish Kaur
S. Rattan Singh Aulakh — Parkash Kaur | **Damaad — Saputry**

Col Pritam Singh
Col Balbir Singh VSM, Arjuna Award winner & Olympian
Prof Popinder Singh Kullar
Helper Joseph Boon. | **Saputar**

14883C

The Statesman – New Delhi 30th Dec 97

Col Balbir bereaved

NEW DELHI, Dec. 29. — Gajjan Singh, a hockey player who in his army days rubbed shoulders with legends like Dhyan Chand and Roop Singh, died here last night, reports PTI.

One of the eminent products of Sansarpur in Punjab, Gajjan (82) led the Indian Army XI (fore-runners of the present Services team) in 1937 and 1946-47.

He is survived by three sons, including Col. Balbir Singh of the 1966 Bangkok Asian Games fame, and two daughters.

Olympians Udham Singh, Tarsem Singh and former India captain Ajit Pal Singh were among the large number of friends and admirers who attended the cremation in Sansarpur today, according to information received here.

The Hindustan Times New Delhi – 30th Dec '97

Gajjan Singh passes away

NEW DELHI, Dec. 29 (HTC) Gajjan Singh, one of the founding fathers of Sansarpur as a nursery of Indian hockey, passed away in the Capital last night.

Gajjan Singh (82) had the distinction of playing alongside legends such as Dhyan Chand and Rup Singh during his Army days between 1934 and 1946.

He was among the people who got the hockey field released from the army for Sansarpur's youngsters and thereby played a significant role in shaping the destiny of Indian hockey. The village Sansarpur on the outskirts of Jalandhar became synonymous with hockey Olympians. Among those groomed by Gajjan Singh to win laurels for India was his son Balbir Singh who is presently the coach of the national women's team.

Olympians Udham Singh, Ajitpal Singh and Tarsem Singh were among the large number of people who attended the funeral at his ancestral village today.

He is survived by three sons and two daughters. One of his son-in-laws is Mr Pritam Singh, a former Director of Sports at Delhi Universi-

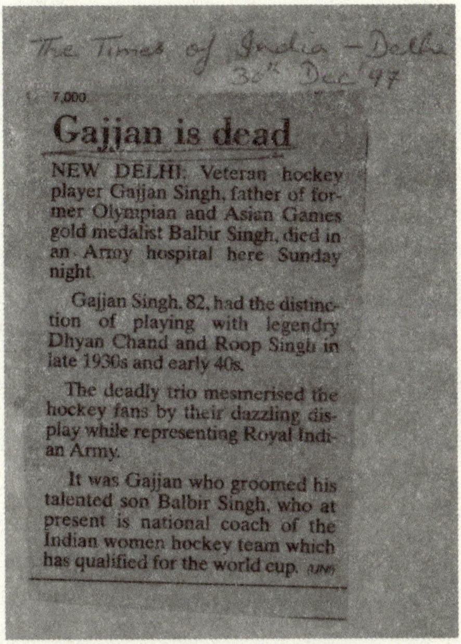

The Times of India – Delhi 30th Dec '97

7,000

Gajjan is dead

NEW DELHI: Veteran hockey player Gajjan Singh, father of former Olympian and Asian Games gold medalist Balbir Singh, died in an Army hospital here Sunday night.

Gajjan Singh, 82, had the distinction of playing with legendry Dhyan Chand and Roop Singh in late 1930s and early 40s.

The deadly trio mesmerised the hockey fans by their dazzling display while representing Royal Indian Army.

It was Gajjan who groomed his talented son Balbir Singh, who at present is national coach of the Indian women hockey team which has qualified for the world cup. (UNI)

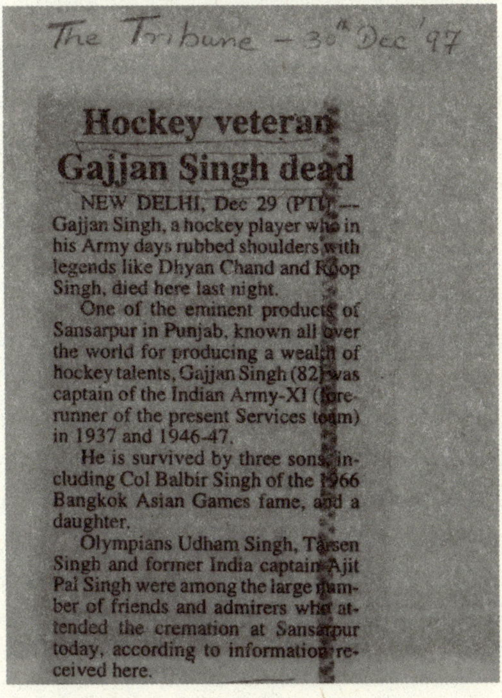

The Tribune – 30th Dec '97

Hockey veteran Gajjan Singh dead

NEW DELHI, Dec 29 (PTI) — Gajjan Singh, a hockey player who in his Army days rubbed shoulders with legends like Dhyan Chand and Roop Singh, died here last night.

One of the eminent products of Sansarpur in Punjab, known all over the world for producing a wealth of hockey talents, Gajjan Singh (82) was captain of the Indian Army-XI (forerunner of the present Services team) in 1937 and 1946-47.

He is survived by three sons, including Col Balbir Singh of the 1966 Bangkok Asian Games fame, and a daughter.

Olympians Udham Singh, Tarsen Singh and former India captain Ajit Pal Singh were among the large number of friends and admirers who attended the cremation at Sansarpur today, according to information received here.

The owner of Haveli restaurant Jullundur, paid tribute to my late father Gajjan Singh by depicting his name on the entrance of the door similar to our house at Sansarpur

My Son—Colonel Sarfraz Singh Kular (PARAS) 4th Generation Soldier from Our Family

I married Surinderjit, daughter of Major Naranjan Singh Sangha on 5 August 1973 at Jalandhar. My marriage was attended by many Olympians and, above all, by Lieutenant Colonel Anant Singh, the hero of Barki and his wife. My daughter was born on 5 September 1974 on Teachers Day.

Colonel Sarfraz Singh, my son, was born on 9 November 1977, the same date when, in 2019, the Dera Baba Nanak corridor was opened for the Gurudwara Kartarpur Sahib.

My son has commanded the 6 Para Regiment with the UN Peacekeeping Forces in Congo. He is a 4th generation soldier from our family in the Indian Army, and he is a mountaineer, a sky diving specialist, a combat freefaller, a river rafting specialist, and a certified scuba rescue diver.

He has scaled the highest peak Mount Everest on 20 May 2018, and he has rich mountaineering experience with the

Hockey Olympian's son wins top adventure award

TRIBUNE NEWS SERVICE

CHANDIGARH, AUGUST 23

Over 50 years after hockey Olympian Colonel Balbir Singh Kular won the Arjuna Award, his son Colonel Sarfraz Singh has received the Tenzing Norgay National Adventure Award.

"I am really proud of him," Kular said of his son. "He has been really passionate about adventure sports and for him to receive such a prestigious award is an honour for the whole family," he added.

Kular, who comes from the famous hockey village of Sansarpur, Jalandhar, was part of the bronze-winning team at the 1968 Olympics. He also won the Asian Games gold in 1966. Kular was honoured with the Arjuna Award in 1968.

His son has received the award in the land adventure category. Sarfraz, 44, is from the elite Parachute Regiment. He got the opportunity to pursue his passion in the Army. In 2004, he climbed his first peak above 7000 metres, and since then, he has climbed over a dozen peaks. He is the director of the National Institute of Mountaineering and Allied Sports (NIMAS) in Arunachal Pradesh.

In 2018, Sarfraz led a mission of eight members to the top of world's highest peak, Mount Everest. In January this year, he led a 40-day, 4,000-km cycling expedition from India to Singapore.

Colonel Sarfraz Singh is a mountaineer, sky diver, combat free faller, river rafting specialist and certified scuba rescue diver.

privilege of scaling several prominent peaks like Mt Nun (7000 M), Mt Trishul, Mt Aconcagua (7040 M) (Argentina), Mt Gorichen, Mt Elbrus (Russia), Mt Kilimanjaro (Tanzania), Mt Harmukh, Mt Stok Kangri, Mt Margherita (Ruwenzori Mountains-Congo), Mt Lobuche (Nepal) & Mt Baisakhi. He is also amongst those few mountaineers from India who could reach the base of Mt Nyegi Kangstang (a virgin 7000 M peak) from Seppa in Arunachal Pradesh. In 2008, he successfully conducted the first-ever International Rafting Expedition of the untamed and technically challenging Kameng River of Arunachal Pradesh. He also led and cycled the First High Altitude MTB Expedition from Bomdila to Bumla Pass (15600 ft), covering a total distance of 300 Km. He has also led the first-ever 4-nation cycling expedition from Manipur to Singapore, covering 4000 Km in 40 days on 23 January 2020. In November-December 2020, he rafted 720 Km of riverine surface of all major rivers of Arunachal Pradesh.

The Secret Behind the Unparalleled Success of Sansarpur

The socio-cultural-economic and educational ethos of Sansarpur must certainly take a large share of the credit for this unparalleled phenomenon. Another crucial factor would have to be its proximity to the Cantonment at Jalandhar. Though little appreciated at the time, the love of hockey was instilled in the villagers by the English Sahibs. At first, they were understandably underwhelmed by the introduction, their life of toll had made them hardy and physically fit. The villagers, always short of avenues for recreation, took to the sponsored game like a duck takes to water. To their delight, they discovered that the Army cantonment, with its splendid sports ground facilities and easy access to the Parade ground, was a rare diversion. Besides, few of the enthusiasts could have failed to see that training imparted by the British cohorts could lead to better job and marriage prospects. All concerned—the British masters, village elders, mothers (especially those with daughters approaching marriageable age), and their wards were

Naik Thakur Singh, the first hockey player from Sansarpur, captained the Army XI which toured New Zealand in 1926 (sitting second from left). Dhyan Chand is sitting on the ground in front of him

more than content with the arrangement. But few anticipated what that tiny seed planted by the British would finally lead to.

The first Indian Army team that visited New Zealand in 1926 had but one player, Naik Thakur Singh Kular from Sansarpur. But this was the opening round of what was to become a torrent of talent from the little hamlet.

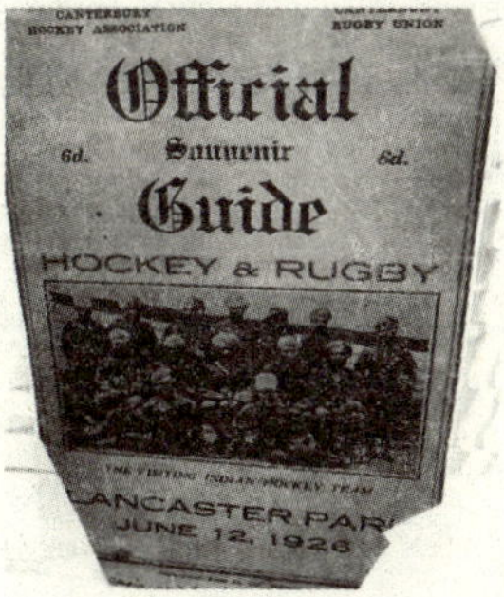

As one success followed another, everyone jumped onto the bandwagon of hockey. Hockey emerged as the sole mantra for worldly success, recognition, and fame. It was hardly surprising, therefore, that parents, family elders, past Olympians and school coaches became walking well-springs of motivation.

If one were to carefully study the environs of Sansarpur, it would be abundantly clear that Sansarpur was not the only village that was close to Jalandhar. There were many other villagers just as close to the cantonment or even closer. But, for reasons unknown, their contribution to hockey was so meagre to be almost nothing before Sansarpur's contribution. The importance of the availability of the ground certainly had a major bearing on Sansarpur's climb from obscurity to glory. No other village had access to such a big field, where hockey could be played with ease. Sansarpur was singularly fortunate in this respect.

The only other village which could have made as significant a contribution as Sansarpur was Khusropur. Here also, as any student of evolutionary biology will appreciate straight away, geographical factors would also seem to have played their part. Khusropur was unfortunate in that it had an open field, which, though small in size as compared to Sansarpur's field, was big enough for hockey. This attenuated the magnetic draw of the cantonment facilities so that although Khusropur's close proximity to Sansarpur was no doubt a motivational factor, the hike to the Jalandhar cantonment seemed less worthy of the time and effort involved in getting there and back. Little did the people of Khusropur realise that what is within easy reach is not always what is best. The Sansarpuris, with no field of their own, were compelled to trek to the cantonment, where, in time, the vast facilities at their disposal gave them a definite edge and ultimately shaped them into world-class players.

Many individuals from Sansarpur took a great personal interest in promoting hockey in the area, prominent among them being Arjun Singh Kular. Physically fleet of foot and a talented all-rounder, he excelled in Hockey, football, and cricket. Though he settled in Kenya, he returned to Sansarpur to spend the remaining years of his life on his native soil. While he was in Kenya, he invited many hockey players from his hometown to visit him. Kenya's loss was soon recouped: Arjun Singh sent some Sansarpur hockey players to Kenya to take up where he'd left off. This was probably the first effort in manpower export that Punjab is so infamous for now, but his pioneering role in providing foreign jobs to Sansarpur hockey players had a tonic effect on Kenyan hockey. Such individual efforts greatly helped in popularising hockey in the initial stage of the Saga of Sansarpur. On their part, Sansarpur parents have made no less a contribution by creating an atmosphere conducive to the sport. In the evenings, the presence of boys within the four walls of the home was a big no-no. Mothers handed their sons tall glasses of milk before peremptorily shooing them out of the house, hockey stick in the hand The husky Sikh lads, ever ready for physical activity and keen to display their skills, needed no second bidding: they made a beeline for the village ground. When they returned, they got another helping of rich, frothy milk in large brass tumblers, but not before they had given their mothers a detailed account of all that had transpired on the field.

Gurmit Singh Kular, the first Olympian from Sansarpur, wants to share a memory with us, so let's hear what he has to say. 'We played for fun and enjoyed the game immensely. In contrast to the delicate youth of today, we were tough men, descendants of mighty battle-hardened warriors. To call us physically fit would be a gross understatement, we did not know what fatigue was. In the evening, after a day's hard labour in the fields, we would eagerly wait for our mother's signal to lope off to the ground to play hockey till it was too dark to see the ball properly. No coke and burgers for us: we slaked our thirst with fresh milk from our milch cattle, and the rich produce of the sweet earth, coupled with toil from sunrise to sunset, turned our bodies to steel. The youngsters of today cannot even walk five kilometres without sitting down to rest their aching legs.'

The fountainhead of meritorious people like Sardar Gurmit Singh Kular, Sardar Gurdev Singh Kular, Late Sardar Udham Singh Kular, Sardar Darshan Singh Tarsen Singh Kular, Balbir Singh Kular, Sardar Ajitpal Singh Kular et al, sprang from hearts of the mothers who were determined to see their sons make something of themselves. Here in lies the secret behind the prodigious talent of Sansarpur hockey players.

Sansarpur's Legacy: Mithapur and Khusropur

Punjab's heritage in the game lives on in the village, which made its dominance felt in Indian hockey, earning global for producing a dozen Olympic medallists from a tiny settlement with nearby villages also benefitting from the hockey culture that spread to adjoining areas specifically, Khusropur and Mithapur were the main beneficiaries.

It gives me pride that the youngsters from Mithapur and Khusropur, Manpreet, Captain of the Indian team, Mandeep and Varun Kumar from Mithapur and Hardik Singh Rai from Khusropur have represented the Indian team in the World Cup 2018 since they grew up listening to the tales of Sansarpur sending a number of players to the Indian team and now they would like to emulate the Sansarpur's golden era by taking forward the Sansarpur legacy.

I can proudly say that we have four players from the belt. They have given hope to many youths that they can have a better life here in their own native place because of hockey. Now, nearby villages are drawing inspiration from Mithapur and Khusropur's success stories and from the Tokyo Olympics 2020, where we won the Bronze Medal and the 1964 Tokyo Olympics, where 4 Sansarpuris won the Gold Medals.

CHAPTER 3

A Hockey Star on the Horizon

The story of hockey begins in the sixteenth century when the earliest forms of hockey emerged across various European countries. While the exact origins remain a topic of debate, it is widely believed that the game evolved from ancient ball-and-stick sports played in ancient Greece, Rome, and Egypt. The roots of this game begin in Egypt, where intricate carvings dating back a staggering 4,000 years immortalise teams brandishing sticks and propelling projectiles with astounding precision.

One of the most significant milestones in hockey's evolution occurred during the eighteenth century in England. All thanks to the bright minds of Eton College—the hallowed institution renowned for its sporting prowess. Some clever students took it upon themselves to establish a precise set of rules and regulations for hockey. With their refined gameplay, they birthed an organised version of the sport that would make any tea-sipping aficionado proud.

The nineteenth century ushered in a transformative era for hockey, forever altering its trajectory across the vast Atlantic. As British settlers ventured to Canada, they carried not just their belongings but an unyielding love for the game.

The late nineteenth century witnessed the birth of international competitions as hockey fever began to sweep across the globe. Driven by the fervour of the British Army, the game began to conquer territories within the British Empire. It is a journey of passion and triumph that unfolded with the arrival of British military officials during the colonial era. In 1885, the Calcutta Hockey Club emerged as the first hockey club, igniting a fervour across the nation. National competitions like the Beighton Cup and Aga Khan tournament captivated the hearts of players and fans, spreading the sport's influence in regions such as Bombay (now Mumbai) and Punjab. The formation of the Indian Hockey Federation (IHF) in 1925, closely following the establishment of the Federation of International Hockey (FIH), cemented India's place in the global hockey community.

1926 marked a turning point in Indian hockey's history as the IHF orchestrated its maiden international tour to New Zealand. In a whirlwind of matches, the Indian men's hockey team displayed their prowess, triumphing in 18 out of 21 battles.

India's profound affection for hockey flourished in the ensuing decades, propelling the nation to unparalleled heights on the global stage. In 1928, the Indian hockey team embarked on a momentous journey, competing in their inaugural Olympic Games. Against all odds, they triumphed, capturing the coveted gold medal in their maiden appearance. This historic victory ignited an extraordinary era of supremacy, with India securing an astounding six consecutive Olympic gold medals from 1928 to 1956. Such an extraordinary feat firmly established India as the indomitable powerhouse of international hockey during that epoch.

Within the annals of Indian hockey, there have been six Balbir Singhs, including me, but there has been only one 'Senior'. It was he who steered the team towards an unprecedented second hat-trick of Olympic gold medals, a triumphant feat accomplished in the years 1948, 1952, and 1956, when India stood tall as an independent nation. This glorious period stands as an indelible milestone, etched forever in India's hockey history.

Sansarpur—that one village, one family, and one street gave India 14 Olympians, an unrivalled track record even today. Take a look at Sansarpur's haul:

Olympic Medals		**Asian Medal**	
Gold	8	Gold	4
Silver	1	Silver	8
Bronze	6	Bronze	1
Padmashri			2
Arjuna Awardee			5
Tenzing Norgay National Adventure Award			1
Maharaja Ranjit Singh Award			4

I am disappointed that the Kulars, the sturdy Jat Sikhs of Sansarpur, never adopted their surname while playing for the country. No one seems to know why. If they had, they would have become world famous. Perhaps it never struck the minds of these Olympians.

Sansarpur—the Nursery of Indian Hockey	
Total Population approximately	4,200
Men folk	2,000
Olympians	14
International Players	19

National Level	90
University Level	54
College Level	120
Member of outstanding teams	90
Military Teams	110

The pioneers included Thakur Singh Kular, who captained the Army XI which toured New Zealand in 1926, followed by Gurmit Singh (Kular), who became the first Sikh in the world to receive the gold medal in the Los Angeles Olympics in 1932. Mexico City 1968 was a record for Sansarpur, where seven of her sons – five doing duty for India, two for Kenya. The five in the Indian team were Balbir (Services) Balbir (Punjab), Tarsem, Jagjit and Ajitpal, and in the Kenya Squad were Hardyal Singh and Jagjit Singh. Much later, Ajitpal Singh Kular of the BSF captained the winning World Cup team in 1975. Others included Gurdev Singh from the Army and Punjab Police, Darshan Singh and Udham Singh from the Punjab Police, and Jagjt Singh and Tarsem Singh from the BSF, all Kulars.

Whenever foreign hockey teams used to visit Jullundur, the organisers of the big match, as a rule, also staged a sideshow in the shape of a game between sides of small Sikh boys, some of them barely as tall as hockey sticks. The youngsters, their hair in neat buns, did not fail to impress the visitors. The boys from the village Sansarpur, a name every Indian hockey fan has known. Talk to anyone from Sansarpur, and the first thing he will claim is that seldom has a hockey team left the shores of India without a Sansarpuri in it. It is like a point of honour with them.

As the earlier tables depicted, the number of Sansarpurians who have played in various tournaments with distinction is mind-boggling, and it shows the parents' role, other family members, Olympians, Ex-Army men and school coaches who were the dominant source of motivation. This clearly reflects the enormous social prestige attached to hockey in Sansarpur.

Except for 1928, 1936, and 1948, Sansarpur always sent one or more players to the Olympic games. This continued till 1988 and missing in 1992 and 1996. Then Bindi Kullar of Sansarpur represented Canada in the 2000 and 2008 Olympic Games, where even India could not qualify. For Sansarpur, it became all the more creditable when the International Olympic Committee Chief, Juan Samaranch, presented the Olympic order to Mr Hardial Singh Kullar at the Olympic Village.

Soldiering and Sports

My official date of birth, as recorded, is 5 April 1945 in Sansarpur, and my hockey adventure commenced as a sprightly member of the Indian Universities Hockey Team, taking my skills all the way to Afghanistan in 1962. It might have been my first tryst out of India, but it was not my first rodeo with hockey.

For any Sansarpur kid, exposure to a hockey field and the first game is a momentous occasion, a kind of ritual bonding, as it were. I was all of four years old then. This is usually the age when children are in lower KG using crayons and plasticine. Subsequent hockey outings were just icing on the cake, each occasion a time for delicious anticipation and recapitulation. I distinctly remember my tryst with big-time hockey. It was when I was nine-and-a-half-years old and when the National Hockey Championship was held in 1956 at Jullundur (now Jalandhar, the eastern segment of the truncated greater

Punjab in India), the country's topmost teams squaring off in a competition for the Rangaswamy Cup. It was an official excuse for an excursion. A fortnight of non-stop excitement! Colourful turbans and new clothes were in evidence everywhere, as the best of Indian hockey talent matched style with skill. Remember, Indian hockey teams were defending Olympic gold medallists in 1948 and 1952 (besides winning in 1928, 1932 & 1936). Hockey was the only sport we were aware of! Shivering with suppressed excitement, I would walk (with as much dignity as I could muster) to the venue, i.e., the PAP (Punjab Armed Police) Jalandhar Hockey Ground, which was three miles from my village. Never were three miles so enchanting a distance. Then the play began, and I would be lost to the world.

It was my great good luck to receive early exposure to the country's best players battling it out in the middle. The result was that, as a Sansarpuri, I was hooked for life, the infection lodging permanently in my system. It was not money, it was not fame or fortune: hockey and hockey alone became my raison d'etre, and I was powerless before its irresistible allure. I knew it would never leave my system.

My destiny then took me on that fateful journey to the Rupa Valley, from where I have begun this book, and the Indian Army seeped into my sinews the same way hockey had, thus making sports and soldiering the two pivots of my life. But we are moving ahead.

Appearance at Lady Hardinge

My association with Lady Hardinge culminated in a love affair in my teens in the 1960s. Providence made me begin my hockey career at Lady Hardinge, and finally, the love affair ended when its name was changed over to Shivaji Stadium.

It is a coincidence that many firsts of my life were played on Lady Hardinge. As long as I played there, Lady Luck smiled at me in winning matches and meeting the Supreme Commander of our Armed Forces, the President of India, but after she changed her name to Shivaji Stadium, the loyalty was divided. To play at Lady Hardinge turf meant everything for me, the love story I had with this lady and the playing on it is unforgettable.

The selection trials for selecting the Combined University were held at Lady Hardinge in June-July 1962 to participate in the Jashan celebration of Afghanistan in August 1962. Being a student of DAV College Jalandhar, I too appeared for the trials and was lucky to put a first step on Lady Hardinge, the famous and my favourite ground. It proved lucky for me as I was selected as the right half for the University team to tour Afghanistan.

Afghanistan Tour 1962

My first foreign tour was with the Indian University Hockey Team to Kabul in 1962. A tour was arranged to participate in the Jashan Celebration, where teams from competing countries had been invited. We had a tough match with the German University Team. Only Inam-ur-Rehman (of Aligarh University) and I went on to represent India at the 1968 Olympic Games in Mexico.

After assembling at Khalsa College, Amritsar, we chugged our way to Attari from where we boarded a train to Lahore, from there we caught the Frontier Mail to Peshawar. The Frontier Mail was a legendary train with an aura to rival that of the fabled Punjab Mail, which ran from Bombay to Peshawar. The Frontier Mail also ran on the Bombay–Peshawar route before Partition. I had the opportunity of seeing Lahore's famous Anarkali Bazaar from a *tonga* with my teammates. All I remember about the bus journey from Peshawar to Kabul was that it was long and tiring. The bus was small, the seats felt rock hard, and the clouds of dust stirred up by the bus's passage over dusty roads penetrated deep into our clothes, luggage, and lungs.

The Khyber Pass is one of those geographical entities that have a near-mythical quality. The pass has been the route of choice for an endless succession of invading armies down the centuries marching in from the rugged northwest.

Dry Fruits and Fruitful Goals

Our bus wheezed its way over the Khyber Pass, neatly taking advantage of the deep valley slicing through the forbidding Hindu Kush Mountain range. Jalalabad, the first town of Afghanistan from the Pakistan border, was warm, and there were fertile crops everywhere. Mounds of oranges and bundles of tall sugarcane were on sale at the outdoor market stalls. Accommodation had been arranged for us in the newly built Kabul Hotel, but we had to take our meals in the obviously named Khyber Restaurant, close to our hotel. It struck me that I was in the land of vineyards, waterfalls, grapes, walnuts and almonds so eloquently and nostalgically described by Zahiruddin Muhammad Babur, founder of the Mughal Dynasty, in his *Baburnama*, as he panted in the sweltering heat of Delhi's fierce summer. There was plenty of dry fruit in evidence everywhere, and I remember bringing back lots of it for my family. This is the place where I developed the habit of bringing back gifts for family and friends. The pack of dry fruits I bought at Kabul was big enough to make even the sturdiest porter quail (dry fruits were expensive in India, even in those days). All our stuff was exempted.

Many years later, when I was touring a foreign country, Balbir Singh of Punjab bought several transistor radio sets but wasn't lucky with the security staff checking the luggage. In those days, a transistor radio set was a rarity, a status symbol as distinctive as today's iPod, iPhones and iPad rolled into one, and attracted heavy customs duty! The next day, to my acute discomfiture, the story was splashed prominently across the front pages of the dailies. All the headlines said the same thing: Balbir of Services (instead of Punjab) held by Indian Customs officials. I contacted the local officer of a newspaper and demanded an apology and a corrigendum. Newspaper editors are unrepentant souls, and this one was no exception. He reluctantly printed a minute apology, tucked away in an obscure corner of the back page to escape detection. The damage had been done.

My National Debut with the Punjab Team in Delhi, 1964

Media reports are like flamboyant tattoos to sportsmen, especially during their formative years. They can choose to either flaunt them or secretly revel in them. Irrespective of the sports or country, sportsmen need an appreciative audience and accolades as much as trees need sunlight, and if someone in their family finds the time and patience to maintain a collection of newspaper and magazine clippings arranged chronologically, so much the better.

I, too, have a personal treasure trove of recollections, the most cherished ones centring around my first Nationals, held at my favourite ground, Lady Hardinge! This was in 1964 when, as already mentioned, I was a student at DAV College, Jalandhar. I was selected as a reserve half-back (centre-half) to Charanjit Singh, who had already played for India in the 1960 Rome Olympics. This hockey great went on to captain the victorious Indian team at the Tokyo Olympics in 1964. It transpired that Charanjit developed some problems with a calf muscle just before the Nationals, so I got the opportunity to make my debut against Bhopal. I think I did well as the centre half, but our team did not click, and the match ended in a draw. In our next encounter with Bhopal, a now-fit Charanjit occupied his usual berth, and our team won the match. I still remember the words written by Ron Hendricks of the Indian Express: 'A little-known Balbir Singh was replaced by Olympian Charanjit.' I had the clipping, and it truly motivated me to do better and play for

India soon and be a part of the winning team. I never got around to saying the words to that splendid sportswriter in person, so I'll say them now: Thanks, Ron, for inspiring me with that article. I think there's a lesson or two in these reminiscences for budding sports writers, foremost among them being their constructive role in encouraging young players to excel. Hendricks was one of the best, God bless his generous heart. His mature wisdom made a positive contribution to many a beginner's career.

My First Hockey Championship in December 1964

I started playing for the Central Command (Lucknow) team, even before joining the Army, as a student at DAV College Jalandhar, as a right half in the Services Hockey Championship held at Lady Hardinge in December 1964. Since I used to play attacking hockey and always on the heels of the forwards, I got an opportunity to score the only goal of the match, my

Central Command team winners of the Services Hockey Championship 1964 with Air Chief Arjan Singh. Balbir can be seen standing third from left

first against great Shankar Laxman in the opening match of the Services Hockey Championship there.

The firstNehru Gold Cup was conducted at Lady Hardinge after the demise of Pandit Jawaharlal Nehru in 1964. I represented the Central Command team in the first Nehru Cup, and the team reached up to the semi-finals.

Nehru Hockey 1965

SIKH REGIMENTAL CENTRE WIN NEHRU HOCKEY

Modan Singh Scores Match-Winner

The Tribune 6 December 1965

I got the opportunity to play for SRC in the Nehru Gold Cup in New Delhi in 1965 after joining SRC Meerut. That was the only time SIKHs could win the glittering trophy, which beat Bombay XI in the final on 5 December 1965. The capacity crowd saw the SIKHs playing for the fourth day running; they scored the match-winner in the sixth minute of the second half of a penalty corner. Left-back Modan Singh of 4 SIKH, with his sizzling hit, beat Bombay GK Bobby Jones hands down. The Late General Harbaksh Singh, GOC Western Command, had witnessed the match and joined the team for the celebration at the 124 TA SIKH officers' mess the very next day on 6 December 1965. Incidentally, the party was also attended by Captain Amarinder Singh, who was the ADC to General Harbaksh Singh and the grandson of Maharaja Bhupinder Singh and son of diplomat royal Yadavindra Singh of Patiala. This was a red-letter day for us when royalty drank rum from the very Nehru cup that the team had won and danced to Bhangra with us. Captain Amarinder Singh is also a former Chief Minister of Punjab and has served on the rolls of 2 SIKH.

The 'Sardars'

Nehru Hockey 1966

I played against my own team in the semi-final as a member of the IHF Red before the Asian Games in 1966. I would like to share with the hockey fraternity and Army personnel that Colonel Gurbaksh Singh, Commandant of the Sikh Regimental Centre at Meerut, stood up to defend the right of the SRC players to play

Col Gurbaksh on the left, Balbir and Haripal Kaushik depicted inthe center, and HC Sareen, Def Secy, on the right

for the regiment regardless of the directive of the federation that National team probables would play for the IHF in the tournament. For him, it was regiment first. The then Defence Secretary Mr HC Sareen, who was also the Vice President of the Nehru Tournament Society, let two players—Balbir Singh

Balbir received the Nehru Cup from Dr Sarvepalli Radhakrishnan, the President of India, twice, for the years 1965 and 1966. In the words of the president of India, 'This young budding lad is in the habit of receiving the Cup every year.'

and Haripal Kaushik—play for the IHF eleven. Eventually, after intervention from the highest quarters, we turned out for the IHF and were later selected to play in the Asian Games. Colonel Gurbaksh Singh told the Nehru Society that he got his orders from the Colonel of the Regiment, Lieutenant General Harbaksh Singh, and not from the Defence Secretary. Haripal Kaushik and Balbir Singh of IHF (Red) made their preordained entry into the final of Nehru Hockey when they prevailed by an only goal over the Sikh Regimental Centre at the Lady Hardinge Ground.

There was more to savour in the aperitif than the meal. IHF Red team succeeded in their attempt to play disciplined and controlled hockey with Balbir (Services) turning in a smart display at the right-half position. They blunted the edge of the more dangerous wing of the SRC team. The capacity crowd was sorry to see the defending Champions go down particularly as two of their stars Haripal and Balbir had played a prominent role in their downfall. 'India's International right-half back Balbir did better by his mistress than his wife, in a manner of speaking,' quipped Mr Ron Hendricks of the *Indian Express*.

National Hockey Championship at Bombay, 1965

I played for Services for the first time in the National Championship, at a time when it was a knock-out tournament, I played only one match for Services against Bengal in the quarter-finals, which we won, but owing to an injury, I could not play in the semifinal against my home team Punjab which we lost with a margin of an odd goal.

Though I played only one game, I was selected for the IHF coaching camp. In this context, I would like to quote the great hockey writer ATP Parthasarathy, who wrote about the semi-final (Services Vs. Punjab) in which I could not play against Punjab.

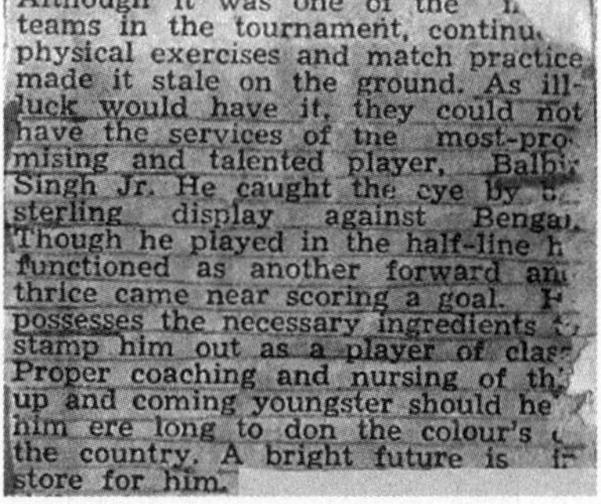
The Services had to blame selves for their lack-lustre di Although it was one of the teams in the tournament, continu physical exercises and match practice made it stale on the ground. As ill-luck would have it, they could not have the services of the most-promising and talented player, Balbir Singh Jr. He caught the eye by sterling display against Bengal. Though he played in the half-line h functioned as another forward and thrice came near scoring a goal. He possesses the necessary ingredients to stamp him out as a player of class. Proper coaching and nursing of th up and coming youngster should he him ere long to don the colour's the country. A bright future is in store for him.

From *Sports and Pastime*, 24 April 1965: 'As ill luck would have it, the Services could not have the services of the most promising and talented player, right half player Balbir Singh. He caught the eye with his sterling display against Bengal. Though he played in the half line, he functioned as another forward and thrice came near scoring a goal. He possesses the necessary ingredients to stamp him out as a player of class. Proper coaching and nursing of this youngster should help him erelong to don the colours of the country. A bright future is in store for him.... A versatile player who is equally at home in the forward line or in the wing-half position, Balbir Singh is a worthy addition to the Services team. Endowed with tireless energy and with good stick work to boot, young Balbir has all the requisites of a top-flight star, which he is fast becoming.'

Sports and Pastime
24 April 1965

National Hockey Championship Final at Poona in 1966: Services Vs. Railways

The Services reached the finals in this tournament, which was played at the Army School of Physical Training in Poona. After some very keen competition up to the semi-finals stage, the Poona National Championship ended on an indecisive note, with Services and the Railways sharing the Rangaswamy Cup following 150 minutes of a goalless draw.

According to Jayee's Spotlight in the *Illustrated Weekly of India*, April 1966, Services, in making the final grade, had the 'find of the tournament' in right half Balbir, a resourceful performer of an attacking order, playing close on the heels of his forwards.

The above photograph of the 1966 Nationals final published in the *Sports & Pastime,* showed 'Services right half Balbir looking anxiously at the umpire after he had kicked the goal-bound try by Railway forward Joginder Singh, who had beaten the goalkeeper Laxman completely.' At that time, my aim was to save the goal at any cost, and being the last defender, I tried to thwart that move. My own 'Hand of God' moment, like Luis Suarez's controversial same in hockey, leg of God! Of course, the umpire awarded the penalty stroke correctly, but it was missed by Mohinder Lal, the right half of the Railways. Fortune favours the brave and the bold!

France Tour – Paris 1966

Prior to the Hamburg International 1966, week-long warm-up matches against France were organised in Paris. The team was accommodated in the National Institute of Sports, where one could find a very conducive atmosphere from a practice point of view.

On one of the off days, a sightseeing of the city was organised for the Indian team, including a visit to the Eiffel Tower after we had visited the Palace of Versailles. We were left to wander on our own but given a specified time to reach the bus. Two of us (Jagjit and I) missed the bus as Jagjit Singh got hooked up by a French girl. We hired a cab with great difficulty due to language problems. On our return to the sports institute, we were reprimanded for being undisciplined. After winning the match series, we were taken to see a show at Falus Berger, the best club in the world. Nightlife in Paris enthralled us. The fair and beautiful skimpily dressed dancers left us astounded and stunned *(sade te hosh hi ur gaye)*. On our return to India, we would narrate these stories, which were often repeated to youngsters after hockey practice in the village. Some youngsters vowed to work hard and get selected for the national team so that they could also visit Europe and see for themselves. It worked as a motivational factor.

Hamburg International May 1966

I was selected to represent the Indian team for the first time in the International Hockey Championship held in Hamburg while I was on the rolls of 4 SIKH.

This was an exciting prospect: I was still in my late teens and ravenous to wear the India jersey. But there was a slight hitch: I was not released in time to attend the training camp at Patiala right on the first day. Thwarted, in an agony of suspense, I wept in frustration in the privacy of my room and prayed for divine intervention. Meanwhile, the IHF had

Winners of Hamburg International Hockey Championship Balbir of 4 SIKH Standing left in the first row with PM Indira Gandhi

been informed that I had reached the camp very late. The next day brought a miracle; my prayers had been answered! The selection committee was asked not to announce the team till my arrival. The selection trials were conducted only after I reached Patiala the next morning, and that too, only for half an hour (just to complete the formalities, I reasoned). When the team was then officially announced, my name was there! I'd been selected despite not having attended the coaching camp! At times, I thought gratefully, God takes matters into His hands.

While travelling by Air India to our first destination, i.e., Berlin, East Germany, we were told that the tour had been delayed for two days as the Indian Hockey Federation had decided to include Balbir of Services in the team. This despite my being selected to play at right half position as a reserve player to legendary Mohinder Lal, who won the 1964 Olympic gold medal for India, his lethal stroke catching the Pakistan goalkeeper flatfooted. The unprecedented development seemed to me to be an example of exceptional foresightedness by a sports federation. That it was the IHF was a very pleasant surprise for me. We in India must learn to repose faith in our youth, no matter what the game. It seems I had come up to everyone's expectations. And so, it came that a young, starry-eyed lad finally realised his dream of representing India! I hugged myself in excitement. Not only was I in the overall squad. I'd finally got the chance to play my first match, that too against East Germany at Jena (the home of the world-famous optics and camera works founded by legendary German lens maker Zeiss), near Leipzig. And since the gods were with me that fateful day on the field, it fell to my lot to score the lone goal of the match a scant 30 seconds before the final whistle... to a thunderous ovation!

As an Army man, it was adequate cause for excitement to visit the place in East Berlin where Hitler stayed during the war, and where he later committed suicide by shooting himself in the temple with his 9 mm Luger as he crouched in his bunker. Why he didn't bite down on the cyanide capsule he always carried is still a mystery. On a more sombre note, I visited the gas chambers that Hitler had built on the outskirts of Jena, where the Nazis had executed thousands of condemned Jews with the help of poison gas. Another memorable visit was to the Berlin Wall, which then divided East and West Berlin, at places even bisecting houses one half in East Berlin, the other half in West Berlin!

My First Match Abroad

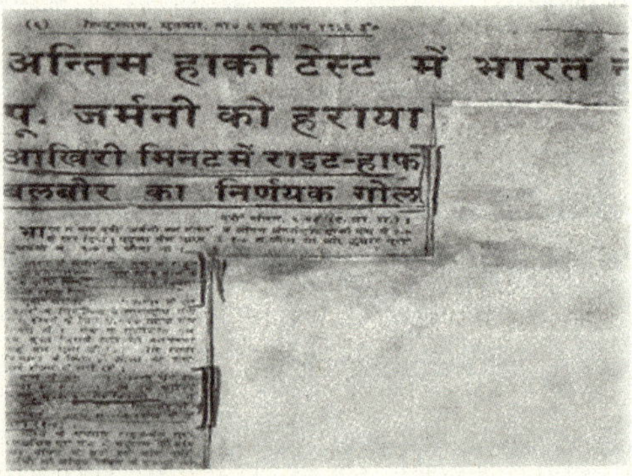

अन्तिम हाकी टैस्ट में भारत

पू. जर्मनी को हराया

आखिरी मिनट में राइट-हाफ

बलबीर का निर्णयक गोल

Venue: Jena near Leipzig East Germany, May 1966, India Vs. East Germany, Score 1-0

The winning goal was scored by me just before the final whistle, the closest win for India with 30 seconds to go. India won the three-test match series with the victory over East Germany in 1966.

Jena was the site of the greatest mass murder of all time, the most infamous Nazi death factory, and the most heinous place on earth where millions of Jews – men women and children were mercilessly put to death in gas chambers, extermination camps or starved to death.

Lucky Shave in Brussels, Belgium, 1966

I was on my first European tour with the Indian team before the commencement of the Hamburg Inter-National Hockey Championship in 1966. We had a tour of Belgium to play a test match against Belgium's National team in Brussels. A day before the match we had gone for shopping to a departmental store very close to our hotel where the Indian team was accommodated. Immediately after we came out of the exit door of the store, a fire broke out on the 6th floor of the departmental store. We were lucky to get out of it but most of them were engulfed in the store, especially on the 6th floor. It was a scene to hear the cries of the people, and we saw them jumping from the 6th floor to save themselves. In the bargain, most of them died on the roadside and some of them inside the store due to suffocation. The fire started at 11.30 AM, and the fire brigade could not control it till late at night due to the congested shopping area. The loss was very heavy in terms of life and property. Being an eyewitness to that I have yet to overcome that scene.

Memories of Japan, September 1966

During the month-long tour of Japan. I played matches in many cities including Kobe, Sapporo, Yokohama, Tokyo, Osaka, Kyoto, Nagoya, and Hiroshima. The team was taken from Tokyo to Osaka by the Shinkansen (as the bullet train was called in the Japanese language), which was the fastest train in the world at that time, and seat belts were compulsory. For those of us who recently moved out of our villages, where life was idyllic and slow-moving, the ride on the bullet train was a novel experience.

After seeing the TV channels and newspapers flash pictures of devastated and ravaged Japan, I recall the Japan I had seen with the Indian team before the March 2011 quake and the tsunami it unleashed. During my visit, around the time, to catch the cherished blossoms turned out to be an experience of a lifetime, which left a lasting impression on me. Notwithstanding the art, culture, and technology of this paradoxical country, what really impressed me were the people. Most of the Japanese do not speak English, and because of their reticence in communicating the foreigners, they often misjudged as being unfriendly. I found them helpful, friendly, polite, and very civil, probably that is why it is safe for a lady to walk alone at midnight, and you will find your wallet where you left it, even hours afterwards. On visiting Hiroshima today, can we believe that it had once been wrecked by a nuclear holocaust? I know that the Japanese are resilient people—they will rise again from the ashes and rubble.

Fifth Asian Games, Bangkok, 1966

In view of the Fifth Asian Games which were to be held at Bangkok in December 1966, the IHF decided to groom me, since Mohinder Lal was not selected for the Japan tour in September 1966. Immediately after the successful Japan tour, the IHF fielded two teams (IHF Red and IHF Blues) in the Nehru tournament in November 1966 to judge the performance of the contenders for the national team.

I was picked to play for IHF Red and Mohinder Lal for IHF Blues, both of us at our respective right-half positions. After the conclusion of the Nehru Cup on 5 November 1966, the players were asked to assemble Jalandhar for the preparatory coaching camp. Mohinder, seized by last-minute doubts about not getting a place in the team, did not join the camp. But exactly one day before the commencement of the final trials, Udham

Singh, former Olympian and Sansarpuri, who happened to be very close to Ashwini Kumar, the IHF chief, reached Delhi to persuade Mohinder to come for the final trials, assuring him a berth in the Indian team. So, Mohinder appeared for the trials and was selected for the team. I was also included in the team but as a reserve halfback to Mohinder. We played our first match in Bangkok against Malaysia, which we won by a solitary goal. Indian coach Randhir Singh Gentle, who had scored the winning goal for India against Pakistan in the final of the 1956 Melbourne Olympics, had taken a positive decision in replacing three of the older players (Mohinder, VJ Peter and Harpal Kaushik) with three youngsters—Balbir Singh (Punjab), Inder Singh (from Railways) and me at right-in, left-in and right half respectively. This gave me the opportunity to play for the national team and paved the way for me to play against Pakistan in the final on 19 December 1966.

The pressure cooker atmosphere matched the frayed tempers in evidence all around us, the hallmark of the epoch-making final. The well-knit Indian team, with nine Sikhs in the first eleven, was given a massive dose of inspiration by none other than the late Prithipal Singh (the great player who had scored 11 goals in the 1964 Tokyo Olympics). Without sounding communal, I can proudly assert that the pride of our *jooris* (top knot) was largely responsible for our victory over Pakistan. Poet Azeezudhin's famous lines came to my mind:

Kise mulkh ya desh di kaum andar,
Jadon hawa azadi di lagdie,
Us Mulkh de Sache ashkan nu
Rehndi hosh na sees te pug di,
Bahute dukh te jo taklif jhallan,
bande kaum de oh daler hunde

Batte ose beri nu bahut painde
jis beni nu bahut ber lagde
Kaid gidra te kavan ne ki hona,
Kaid pinjre bazz te sher hunde.'

(When the winds of independence blow through the blood of any race or nation, to the true patriots of that country, neither head nor turban matters. Ready to face difficulties, they are the pride of their country. Only that jujube tree has stones hurled at it, which bears sumptuous fruit. There is no point in imprisoning crows and jackals, only falcons and lions are fit to be imprisoned.)

These immortal lines are a prime motivating factor, inspiring the present generation of hockey players of the country to go and earn better results. I cannot describe the emotion, the pride, that comes with seeing the Indian tricolour unfurled after a victory. Suddenly, everything makes complete and utter sense: the gruelling training, the rigorous selection camps, and the year of pain that seems as nothing before that piece of tricoloured fabric triumphantly swaying in the breeze.

The Golden Goal

It transpired that I was able to position myself so advantageously as to be instrumental in initiating a delightful move for my namesake from the Railways to administer a classic finishing touch to give India the first Asian Gold Medal.

This is what teamwork is all about. We gave ourselves the Gold Medal by working as a team. For the first time in the history of the Asian Games Hockey Championship, the Indian National Anthem was played during the presentation ceremony as I stood on the top step of the podium along with the other ten players, moist-eyed. I saw the tricolour being unfurled at the hockey stadium in Bangkok, probably our most dominant victory over Pakistan. **I cannot describe the emotion, the pride in becoming the First Asian Gold Medallist in Hockey from the Sikh Regiment.** It was a great honour, and this win made it more special. If you were to ask me what the ingredients of success are, I would say that discipline, respect for seniority and authority, hard work, sacrifice, constant practice, single-minded focus on the ultimate objective, mental and physical conditioning and above all, love for the country.

Tomorrow, God is not going to ask you what you dreamed, what you planned, or what you preached. He is going to ask what you did. I can say with pride that I was a part of the winning team which got a Gold Medal for my country.

I believe that as a longtime admirer and lover of hockey and *fauj*, the Indian Military is one of our most inspiring institutions. I love hockey, the Indian Army, my national anthem, and my country.

This was an epochal event, and it will be remembered in the history of Indian hockey forever.

This is what teamwork is all about

The final line-up against Pakistan was as under:

Goalkeeper – Shankar Laxman (Captain)

Full-Backs, Keeper – Gurbux Singh, Prithipal

Half-Backs – Balbir Services, Jagjit Singh, A Frank

Forwards – Balbir (Railways), Balbir (Punjab), Harbinder Singh, Inder Singh, Tarsem Singh

It is rare that four Kulars from Sansarpur played in the final against Paksitan.

The Golden Stamp

To commemorate India's resounding victory over Pakistan in the final of the Fifth Asian Games in Bangkok, the Indian Postal Department brought out a special stamp of

Balbir is the only sportsman from the Sikh Regt depicted on the stamp

Four Players Pictured on the stamp ,Balbir,Vinod,VJ Peter,Mukhbain

Out of the four only Balbir had the Privilege to

play the final of Asian games Bangkok December 1966

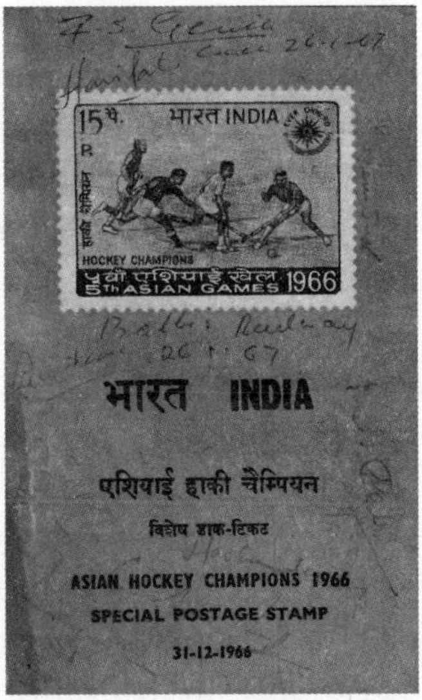

15 paisa denomination. The monochromatic blue coloured stamp shows four hockey champions playing the game of hockey in shorts and T-shirts. Two of these players are recognisably Sikhs with their buns (top knots) tied in a *rumal* (handkerchief-sized material), a common way of covering the head.

The most compelling part of the visual is the obvious diehard spirit of the players to win the match. The First Day Cover shows the emblem of the Fifth Asia Games represented by a full rising sun with the slogan 'Ever Onward' written within the circle. The cancellation shows a hockey stick as a distinctive mark.

I must reveal the real story behind this stamp. The picture was selected from a photograph snapped by a lensman from *Sports & Pastime* during the Nehru Hockey final between IHF Red and IHF Blue at the Lady Hardinge Stadium on 5 November 1966 and published in *Sports & Pastime (a Hindu* publication). It has added significance for me since I not only figured on the stamp, but I was also a member of the Indian team that won the Asian Games gold in Bangkok one month later, on 19 December 1966.

Punjabi Sensibility Unplugged at Lahore

'Mian kiddi bumb Aslam Sher de ya.'

At the Qaid-e-Azam International Hockey Tournament in Lahore in 1976, India Vs. Poland, the game was in full progress. In one of the attacking moves by the Polish team, a skirmish ensued between Aslam Sher Khan and a Polish player who tried to reach the ball, but accidentally, his hockey stick got hooked in Aslam's skimpy shorts. Aslam strove forward to intercept the ball, resulting in a long tear revealing his bums to the spectators. When he ran, the flaps bellowed like a skirt that kept the audience entertained for a short time, much to the ignorance of Aslam. Hearing the shouts, claps, and remarks of the Pathans and Khans, the umpire stopped the match. The Indian side encircled Aslam while he changed into another one. He became the laughing butt of all the players. It was after this incident that the players started carrying spare shirts and shorts. *'Mian kiddi bumb Aslam Sher de ya,'* blurted the spectators while watching the match. Punjabi sensibility has sprung up many a time during the hockey matches. One really does not know what exactly it stands for, but since it is doing the social rounds, exploring what constitutes 'Punjabi sensibility' might not be a bad idea.

Madurai National Championships, 1967

'Give me Joginder, Peter and Balbir Singh of Services on the right side, and I will defy the entire world.'

—Jimmy Nagarwala, Chairman Selection Committee IHF and former IG of Gujarat Police, quoted in the *Indian Express,* 14 March 1967.

It was during the Madurai National Championships that, for the first time, I had to play as left half, a position I had never played in before. This was even though it was common knowledge that I was more comfortable at the centre-half or right-half positions from where I could go into attack mode in support of the forwards. At the same time, I could fall back swiftly, seamlessly switching to defence and even defend the goal if the goalkeeper was beaten.

Looking back today, I am amazed that I was able to be all over the place, donning different caps, as it were, as I went from attack to deep defence. But I was crazy about hockey and just couldn't help myself; I just had to be where the action was. And since it worked out well, no one was heard complaining! Jimmy Nagarwala, as quoted above, also said that the three players, from the right flank of the Indian team, were the most formidable trio available anywhere (apart from the divine Trinity, I suppose). Jimmy Nagarwala's statement is an unbelievable compliment indeed. Given that he had a plethora of players to choose from, what made him say with so much confidence that these three players on the right flank were all that he needed to take on the entire world?

Players Discipline the Disciplinarians! Egypt Tour, 1967

Hockey players were always India's premier sporting stars, a fact that was quite evident from their carriage. Cockiness was the first sign of defiance of authority, i.e., the team officials and administrators touring with them.

Prior to the Madrid international tournament, the team went on a tour to Europe and Egypt under the captaincy of Prithipal Singh. We reached Cairo, where we had to play a test match. Accommodation was provided in the stadium itself. The result would be a foregone conclusion, but our game strategy had still to be made, and all of us had to assemble at 9 pm in the skipper's room, without exception. Defaulters would be thrown out of their rooms. It later transpired that right after evening practice, RP Mehra, the manager, coach RS Gentle and umpire Sarosh Nagarwala had sneaked out of the stadium without informing the team captain and without having dinner with the team. They went to the main centre shopping complex; maybe it was a pleasure jaunt or to a nightclub. Meanwhile, all players made it to the meeting, but the said officials were nowhere to be found.

A grim-faced Indian skipper announced at 11 pm that the main entrance to the complex (where the team was residing) would remain sealed until further notice. The unsuspecting trio returned long after midnight. But with the gates not being opened for them, they had no choice but to stand shivering outside in the biting cold. We could hear their screams behind them to a man. Jagjit Singh (Jagga), my roommate, was a jovial character and would repeat their pleas in a female voice that came clearly in the silence of the night, with our delighted laughter echoing in the empty stands of the stadium that would soon be packed within a few hours. Finally, the erring officials realised that the players were not going to budge.

It was 6 am when stadium attendants opened the gates that they were able to enter. No one spoke of it at the breakfast table, but the silence—more eloquent than a thousand words—conveyed the importance of discipline to the discipliners. After we won the match, all was sorted out amicably, thanks to the delicious Indian food sent by the only Indian family living there. The team was taken sightseeing to the famous Pyramids in Giza, where I also saw many mummies and the age-old Sphinx.

Bhangra—Flamenco with the Senoritas

At times, we international players led charmed lives. One such instance was our trip to Spain in 1967. Though it was just another tour for us, the Spaniards were flabbergasted seeing us. Most of them had never encountered a Sikh, what to peek of a dozen plus strapping, sun-tanned Sardars! It was obvious that they would never forget the sight of us-lean, wiry, bronzed, manned and bearded like lions!

We were told that the local girls were fascinated by our mannerisms, and the sight of tall, husky, martial-looking turban-clad men left them dumbstruck. To tell the truth, the language barrier never really hindered our chances of getting lucky on that tour! There were some hilarious moments when the Punjabi *mundas* tried wooing the Spanish girls. It goes to the credit of the senoritas that they responded with delight. They were especially fascinated by the way we Sikhs combed our hair in reverse, back to front, before making the bun with a deft twist of our steely wrists.

The beautiful Spanish girls practically lined up to date these good-looking, manly men from the mysterious Orient. We were probably living characters straight out of the pages of Aladdin and Ali Baba to them. The denouement is truly fascinating, but that is another story. The people of Madrid and Barcelona had never seen a Sikh (player or otherwise) with a turban on his head. We must have been as alien to them as Martians. Sometimes, when we would come out on the balcony of the hotel to comb our long hair, passers-by would stop and gape at us in awe and wonder. It was all very strange and fascinating for them. They would gape at us as we twisted our long hair into buns on our heads and tied a handkerchief around them.

Madrid, 1967

There were 14 Sikhs in our 18-member team, so you can imagine the impact we made. Most of us did not know either English or Spanish, so we got hold of an interpreter to transcribe in Hindi a few sentences in Spanish, such as 'I love you' or 'You look beautiful' and slipped the chits into our pockets. These 'cheat sheets' came very handy when we had to make short conversations with the dazzling Spanish girls. To the brave go the spoils of war, though the girls weren't exactly fighting us off; quite the contrary, in fact.

The Indian hockey team was invited for dinner before the final, by India's Ambassador to Spain, Raja Swai Man Singh of Jaipur, a great polo player who later died on horseback while playing polo in London. He was the father of Brigadier Bhawani Singh, who was the Adjutant at the Indian Military Academy as a Major, and the husband of the beautiful lady Shrimati Gayatri Devi. When we entered the anteroom for the party, I saw the photograph of Shrimati Gayatri Devi, who was not in Spain at that time, but she really impressed me, and I have not seen a more beautiful and elegant lady in my life.

While the party was in full swing, I was called by Mr Ashwini Kumar, IHF chief, on the sidelines, who asked me to play at the left half position in the last two matches of the championship just to adjust Mohinder Lal at the right half position. I was reluctant in the beginning and requested the IHF chief to put Mohinder Lal as the left half and not to shift me from my original position, which I had earned, showing my worth on the playing field, but the IHF chief was very firm in his decision, and I had to agree with him. However, I laid a condition that for the team's sake, I would play at the left half position only for the remaining two matches, but I should not be asked to play at that position during the European tour, which was to follow after the Madrid international competition. I played the last two matches in the left-half position in place of Harmek Singh, and we won the Gold Medal against Spain 'A' team by one goal to nil.

I cannot forget a huge opportunity I missed in the first half of the final. India was awarded a penalty stroke, and I was assigned to take it. Guess who the goalkeeper was who stood before me? It was none other than the later International Hockey Federation (IFH) chief, Leandro Negre! But something went horribly wrong: I didn't connect with full force, the stick merely glanced off the ball. I had never seen such a rotten penalty shot, let alone made one! Both of us stood stunned as the ball rolled weakly and stopped just in front of Negre. It was exactly like one of those frustrating near-miss golf putts you see on TV, the ones that roll straight towards the cup run out of steam midway and come to rest right on the lip of the cup! During the 2010 World Cup in Delhi, I narrated this incident to Negre, and we had a hearty laugh. In Madrid, the team was taken to see a bullfight. It was captivating and repulsive at the same time; the matador was graceful and killed the bull finally, but we Indians are against killing bovines, I guess, so we came away from the arena with mixed feelings of awe and disgust. I saw another side of Spanish nature when we were driven out into the countryside to a ranch where young bulls were bred. The Spanish team jumped into the enclosed arena and had a field day playing and dodging the feisty young bulls. I found it easy to believe the stories I'd heard about Pamplona, the Spanish town where men allow bulls to chase them through the streets, often with fatal results. There seems to be something in the hot Latin blood, a possible legacy from the extinct Cretan culture, that challenges young men to test their potency against the ultimate symbol of masculinity—a powerful young bull. Kerala also does the same type of practice on one of their festivals.

Dutch Drubbing, 1967

After the Madrid tournament, we had a match in Amsterdam against Holland, where the coach asked me to play as the left half. I almost begged him to let me play at the right half, but he was firm in his decision. Maybe it was a mistake not to see how effective a player can be in a particular position. I was playing way under my potential in that unfamiliar position.

From Amsterdam, the team flew to Berlin to play against West Germany. Gentle, our team coach, again asked me to play as the left half. Since the team had lost to Holland, I suggested to him that both Mohinder Lal and I should be tried out at both positions, with me playing at right half in the first half, and thereafter as the left half. The opposite arrangement could be made applicable to Mohinder. Gentle agreed to the proposal, but we again lost 1-3. This was Germany's first victory against India, and famous hockey coach Paul Lissek played in this match at left half position. It fell to my lot that, playing in the left-half position, I was to score the lone goal for India, a goal that is memorable for me as this match was played in the main Olympic stadium where the 1936 Olympic Games were held, the very Games where Hitler slipped away so as to avoid giving four gold medals to the black athlete who had single-handedly demolished the Fuehrer's theory of Aryan supremacy—the great Jesse Owens. The World Cup football final was also played in the same stadium in the year 2006.

The point I'm trying to make here is that I was so sure

of my berth in the team that I could afford to dictate my terms...backed by suitable reasoning, of course! I was selected to represent India in the Sri Lanka tournament of July 1967 and the pre-Olympics in London in October, but the Army authorities did not release me since I was undergoing officer training at the Military Academy. I was quite a certainty with the team and badly wanted to visit the Emerald Isle, famous as the location where the epic Hollywood war movie *The Bridge on the River Kwai* was shot (the actual story was about the dank, leech-infested jungles of Thailand). My Command had informed IHF that during my training period, I would only be released for the Olympic Games, not for international competitions. I took the decision in my stride. I was in the Army, after all. Orders are orders! After 50 international travels, my heart still longs for my first trip to Sri Lanka

The Bridge on the River Kwai

Col Sarfraz had the privilege to cross the historical World War II bridge on cycle near the Burma-Thailand border in January 2020

CHAPTER 4

The Road to the Olympics

Pre-Olympic Tour to East Africa, 1968

For those who are not aware of it, I'd like to mention that the average altitude of Kenya's western highlands is 2,000 meters. This is a beautiful region of high green mountains and precipitous valleys populated by people who arguably have the most prodigious stamina in the world. The rural people are herders who spend all day with their livestock and return home as fresh as if they'd gone for a walk in the neighbourhood park. It is no wonder, then, that Kenya, like Ethiopia before it has produced a steady stream of marathon champions. To make things tougher for us, many Indians have settled in Kenya, and competition with the tireless locals has added a new dimension to their hockey skills.

Under the circumstances, even we hardy Sikhs, as well as others in the Indian team, were obviously badly in need of stamina enhancement training. And what better place for that than the Nilgiris range of hills? After receiving high-altitude training at Lawrence School, Lovedale, situated near the picturesque hill station of Ootacamund in the Nilgiris, the team left for a tour of Kenya and Uganda at the end of August 1968. Very tough competition awaited us, especially from the Kenyan team. The hard-pressed Indians lost the first match to Kenya in Nairobi, where I played as a left half. Quickly reassessing the situation, the management asked me to return to my original position as the right half in the second test. This time, we won by two goals to one. I had the good fortune of scoring the winning goal from the top of the circle atthe inside-left position, that too on the wrong foot. A different ballgame!

Our time in Africa flew by. We were kept so busy that it was almost like the frenetic scene at home. There were the usual practice sessions with the team, but off the field, it was a different ball game altogether. We were invited to put up with the locals, most of whom were immigrants from India. We obliged, and what followed was a matter of shame to the team's integrity. Some players ended up mingling with the locals to the extent that after a point, we ended up indulging in a lot more than just fun. Maybe it was an adrenaline rush or the loneliness of being so far away from home, or plainly liquor, but whatever the cause, we ended up losing the first match of the series, our pride and most of us, our dignity. What started as a candlelit, laughter-filled evening of friendship and warmth that was supposed to be banked in our memories and hauled out happily at a later date to cherish and talk about gleefully ended the next morning on the field with our heads low. After completing the tour of these countries, though, we reached Mexico City in the first week of Oct 1968.

Making the Olympic Team was a Big Goal

I am lucky to have represented my country in the Olympic Games before the major injury to my knee; otherwise, I would have missed not being known as an Olympian.

The Olympic Games have become so global that top sportsmen of different sports like Tiger Wood, Roger Federer, and Rafael Nadal would like to be a part of it.

Gurmit Singh Kular made it to the Olympics in 1932 in Los Angeles. After that, all the young players in the village of Sansarpur wanted to become Olympians. As we say, confidence sometimes comes from within and surroundings. We started doing amazing things due to the competition with the senior players and could watch them and say: 'If they could do it, we can do it.' That's the reason we could produce so many Olympian/International hockey players from Sansarpur. So, reaching there is a great extension of one's storied sporting career. Udham Singh Kular, a player of Dhyan Chand's calibre, for whatever reasons, never got the recognition he so richly deserved. Submerged under the waves of history, he did not receive the same adulation. He played in the 1952, 1956, 1960, and 1964 Olympics, winning three Gold and one Silver Olympic Medal.

Olympian Gurmit Singh Kular, the first player in the world who played hockey with a turban in 1932 while on the European tour before the 1932 Olympics

Mexico Olympic Games 1968

I did not play the 1968 Nationals at Ooty as I was undergoing the officers' training at the Indian Military Academy. Mr Ashwani Kumar, the IHF Chief requested the Chief of Army Staff to arrange to make me available for the Indian Hockey Team for the Mexico Olympic Games.

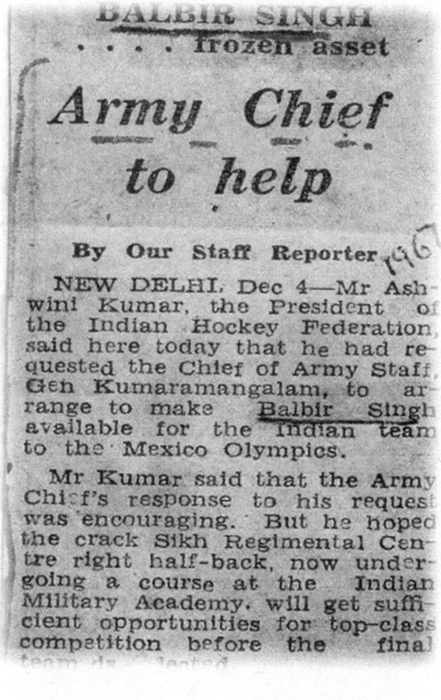

BALBIR SINGH
. . . . frozen asset

Army Chief to help

By Our Staff Reporter 1967

NEW DELHI, Dec 4—Mr Ashwini Kumar, the President of the Indian Hockey Federation, said here today that he had requested the Chief of Army Staff, Gen Kumaramangalam, to arrange to make Balbir Singh available for the Indian team to the Mexico Olympics.

Mr Kumar said that the Army Chief's response to his request was encouraging. But he hoped the crack Sikh Regimental Centre right half-back, now undergoing a course at the Indian Military Academy, will get sufficient opportunities for top-class competition before the final

Mr Kumar said that the Army Chief's response to his request was encouraging. But he hoped that his crack Sikh Regimental Centre right half-back would get sufficient opportunities for top-class competition before the final team was selected.

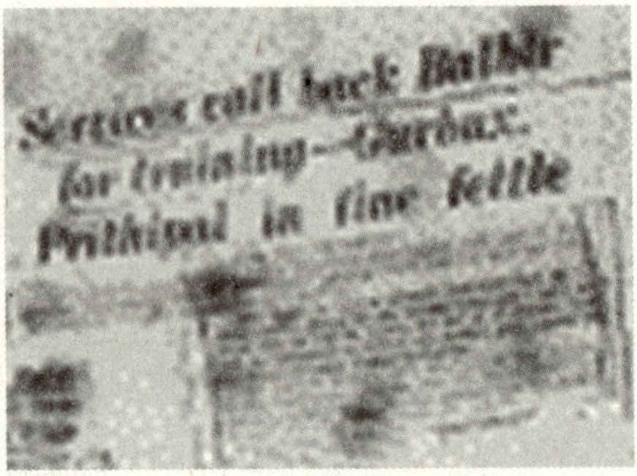

Services call back Balbir for training—Gurbax: Prithipal in fine fettle

I could not make myself available for the final Selection Trials for the Mexico Olympics-bound team due to my officers' training. Balbir Singh, the sturdy and rugged half-back of the Sikh Regiment, would miss the two-day trials at Jalandhar due to his officers' training, too. But Balbir was such a splendid halfback that he was an automatic choice for any Indian team, and I had no doubt that he would be among the list of 18 players that would be nominated to defend our hockey gold medal at the Mexico Olympic Games in October 1968.

Mr Ashwini Kumar, IHF Chief, has told the Press that the Army Chief had agreed to release Balbir for the next camp and matches and that the selected team would play at Lovedale Lawrence School the next month.

Mexico Olympics Hockey Team

The team was announced on 18 July 1968 after the two-day trials at Jalandhar, which was welcomed and described as a team of talent, tact and great confidence.

The opening Ceremony of the 19th Olympiad at Mexico City was conducted at the newly built Azteca Stadium with much fanfare on 12 October 1968. It was a memorable day for the Lucky Seven Sanarpurians. Five of them were doing duty for India, and two for Kenya. Before the Olympic flame was lit, the historic photograph of the lucky seven hockey players from Sansarpur was taken in the Stadium.

All the Kulars at the Opening Ceremony of Mexico Olympics Azteca Stadium on 12 October 1968

Balbir at Azteca Stadium Mexico City

Balbir and Prithipal Singh, Captain of the hockey team holding the National Flag at Azteca Olympic Stadium Mexico

Mexico: Warm-up match: India Vs. Australia 9 Oct 1968

Reuters Report:
Olympic Champions India played out a 1-1 draw with reigning bronze medal holder Australia on 9 Oct 68 before the commencement of the Olympic Hockey Games. In this match, India scored through the right half, Balbir Singh, but later conceded the equalising goal to Pearce.

Opening Match: India Vs. New Zealand at the Mixhuca Hockey Ground

New Zealand sparked off a major shock at the Olympic tournament by beating India, the World and Olympic champions, with a 2-1 win in the opening match.

Prior to this, India had lost only one game in the Olympics to Pakistan, that too in the Rome Olympics final in 1960. The winning goal was then scored by Nasir Bunda, inside-left of Pakistan, in the 11th minute of the first half. This final was played in the football stadium instead of the Marble Hockey Stadium in Rome. In the game with New Zealand, I blamed myself for not scoring a goal from a penalty stroke in which I hit the goal post, and Prithipal also had countless chances from penalty corners in the second half but was repeatedly penalised on almost every occasion due to the new stick rule.

India Vs. West Germany 11 October 1968

India Vs. Japan 20 October, Mixhuca Ground Mexico City:

Since the 1936 Berlin Olympics, Germany had caused us a few hiccups on the hockey field, and on 11 October, we again fought desperately and at times ferociously to overcome a strong West German team in a do-or-die game.

India's winner came late in the second half when right-half Balbir converted a goal with a powerful scoop and sent the ball home after receiving a neat pass from left-back Prithipal after we had been awarded a short corner for sticks by Klaus Greinert. The next match against hosts Mexico on 15 October was a cakewalk. As Reuters reported: 'India swamped newcomers Mexico 8-0 in the third match of the Olympic Hockey Tournament. Centre-forward Harbinder scored a hat-trick, left-back Prithipal got two goals and right-half Balbir (Services), centre-half Ajitpal and inside-left Inder Singh got one each.' The results of the other games that India won were as follows:

India Vs. Belgium: 2-0
India Vs. Spain: 1-0
India Vs. Japan: 5-0
India Vs. East Germany: 1-0

Never Before, Never Since

India's penultimate and crucial match against Japan in the Tournament ended abruptly and sensationally when the Japanese team walked out of the field in protest against a British umpire's decision.

Japan had been defending desperately throughout and had managed to keep their goal intact against some terrific India pressure. When the British umpire AH Young awarded a penalty stroke against them in the 55th minute, the Japanese complained bitterly against this decision, but when Mr Young refused to change his decision, they walked off the field led by their skipper Matsumoto. After the team walked off the field, the British umpire asked the Indian team to take the penalty stroke to complete the formality as per hockey rules of that time. I stepped forward to take that unique penalty stroke, and I put the ball into the empty goal, and Mr Young pointed towards the centre, thus awarding the goal and the match to us. Since this was a league match of pool 'A', it was decided by the panel of the jury to award five goals, which had never happened in the history of the Olympic Games. Japan thus conceded the match to India, and with two more points from the game, we consolidated our position at the top of the pool table.

Therefore, I was credited for putting the ball into the empty goal and getting five goals in return for the Indian team—never ever heard in the annals of the game.

A half-back never stands as tall as when he kneels to help the forwards

However, recently, the Federation of International Hockey (FIH) has issued an instruction that in case such an incident occurs again, all the teams playing in that pool will be given five goals and three points each against the defaulting team.

India Back on Gold Trail: India Vs. Australia Semifinals 23 October 1968

Captain Prithipal and Balbir of Services on the Injured List

Despite our shock defeat at the hands of New Zealand, we once again were back on the medal trail. Having won all the remaining matches in the pool 'A', we qualified for the semifinals.

As *Reuter* reported on 15 October 1968:

'A tough tussle was expected in the India Vs. Australia tie in the semifinals. Olympic champions India had two key players, Captain Prithpal Singh and right-half Balbir of Services, on the injured list. Prithipal had badly bruised his calf muscle, and right-half Balbir (Services) had a sprained ankle during India's tough contest with East Germany in the last encounter of the pool "A".'

INDIA SHOCKED BY AUSTRALIA

Extra-time goal decides rip-roaring semi-final

Kenya, Kiwis beaten

There was an indication that the India Vs. Australia semi-finals would be a very close and exciting battle. India failed to reach the final, and disaster duly struck. The *Reuters* report dated 23 October best sums up the Indian fade out:

'India failed to make it to the Olympic hockey final for the first time since 1928. Former Olympic champion India's hopes of retaining the hockey gold were ground to dust by Australia. India took the lead in the 14th minute when right-half Balbir (Services), India's great penalty marksman, stepped into the penalty spot and scored.

'Brian Glencross, the Australian right-back, cracked home the equaliser in the 17th minute of the second half, and Australia's winning goal came two-and-a-half minutes before the end of extra time, from a penalty corner smacked into the Indian goal again by the sharpshooter Brain Glencross.'

For Indian hockey, however, 23 October 1968 was the saddest day ever. It was also a chilling foretaste of things to come....

In The Middle of the first Dope Tests in the World of Hockey

DOPE TEST

Two players from In[illegible] and Australia hockey [illegible] had to undergo drug te[illegible] after their historic sem[illegible] finals on Thursday.

This is the first time th[illegible] has been done in the Olym[illegible] pic Hockey Tournament.

The strict anti-doping re[illegible] gulations produced their fir[illegible] offender when Sweden ha[illegible] its bronze medal for th[illegible]

Dope tests in the context of hockey were introduced for the first time at the Mexico Olympics. Since I was limping throughout the match due to pain in the sprained ankle, VJ Peter and I, who played the right-in position, had to undergo a test after the semi-final. We were very nervous and unaware of the consequences. Peter kept nudging me every minute, asking anxiously, 'What's going to happen now?' That is the only time I remember Peter being nervous… a far cry from the Peter we knew on the hockey field- supremely confident, sure-footed and agile. Both of us were cleared as the tests did not reveal that anything was amiss.

A Consolation Bronze Meal

Two days later, after a keenly fought battle, India won their playoff match against West Germany 2-1 to earn the bronze medal—a poor consolation indeed after being shut out for the first time in Olympic history, from having a shy at the coveted gold in the title round. The winning goal was scored by Balbir of Railways.

Prime Minister Indira Gandhi's Remarks

The humiliation caused an uproar at home. Prime Minister Indira Gandhi, according to a PTI report dated 25 October from Patna, attributed India's defeat by Australia in the semi-finals to a lack of discipline and single-minded purpose. She thought that the people of some other countries had shown a greater sense of discipline as compared to the Indians.

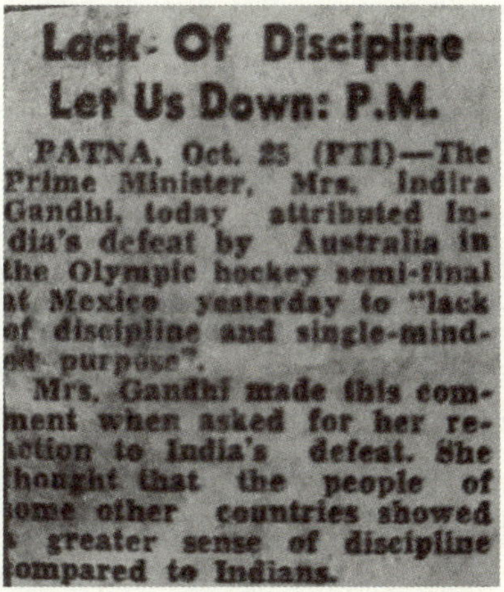

Lack Of Discipline Let Us Down: P.M.

PATNA, Oct. 25 (PTI)—The Prime Minister, Mrs. Indira Gandhi, today attributed India's defeat by Australia in the Olympic hockey semi-final at Mexico yesterday to "lack of discipline and single-minded purpose".

Mrs. Gandhi made this comment when asked for her reaction to India's defeat. She thought that the people of some other countries showed a greater sense of discipline compared to Indians.

However, Raja Bhalindra Singh, Chef-de-Mission of the contingent at Mexico City, thought it was a mixed bag (as reported in the *Free Press Journal*, 30 January 1969: 'The Raja praised only Ajitpal and Balbir of the Services in the half-line, and both the full-backs, Prithipal and Gurbux. The goalkeeper did not perform as well as expected, and this shook the confidence of the team. The forwards did not function effectively as a combination, though there were flashes of individual brilliance.' IHF president Ashwini Kumar's analysis of India's lacklustre performance read as follows (*The Tribune*, 5 November): Inadequate facilities, less coaching time, injured right-half Balbir and left-half Harmeek, etc.

What Went Terribly Wrong—My Take

I fully agree with the statement made by Prime Minister Indira Gandhi that India lost to Australia because of a lack of discipline and single-minded purpose. India's Iron Lady had unerringly pinpointed the main reason for the downfall of Indian hockey, a malady for which the IHF has still to find a remedy. In my mind, the main reason for India's debacle was the appointment of two captains, the biggest blunder committed by the IHF. It resulted in groupism in the team and undermined discipline. The control factor was missing nobody wanted to listen to anyone. This point—joint captains—was most crucial as it was the genesis of all the other problems. The IHF is squarely to be blamed for writing a dubious paragraph into the recorded books of Indian hockey by selecting two skippers for the Olympic team. The baffling move fragmented the team by creating competing factions.

The biggest victim of this unhappy decision was team spirit. Both the captains were at loggerheads with each other, an outcome which created confusion in the minds of players and killed Indian Hockey. Yet, despite all these odds, the team qualified for the semis because it had the talent and depth needed to win the gold. However, in its hobbled condition, it was lucky to even win the bronze. The meeting to appoint a captain for the Mexico-bound team took place at Lawrence School, Lovedale, in the Nilgiris Hills. Prithipal was selected as captain based on merit and seniority. This ran afoul of Gurbux Singh of Bengal, who, it must be remembered, was very junior to Prithpal. Gurbux issued a threat that he would leave the camp if he were not appointed joint Captain, and this asinine suggestion got the nod from Ashwini Kumar This was a turning point for the team's fortunes at the Games. As such, there is no way out but to load the onus for India's loss squarely on the shoulders of the IHF, much more so than Gurbux, who was playing an opportunistic card. With him and Prithipal wrestling for control, indiscipline and groupism flourished so that the car of the Indian hockey team careered out of control and ended up in the ditch. Ultimately, not the team alone but every Indian had to pay the penalty. Gurbux, as a result, became very unpopular among the Indian players during the tour and Olympic Games.

Finals of the Mexico Olympics

I watched the finals while sitting between two great sports personalities—Raja Bhalindra Singh, President of the Indian Olympic Association (IOA) and Mr Ashwani Kumar, the Chief of IHF. Even after winning the Bronze Medal, the entire hockey team was in a sad mood while watching the proceedings of the final match between Pakistan and Australia since this was the first final where India could not figure in Olympic hockey history.

During the interval of the finals, I was called by Mr Ashwani Kumar and was asked to sit between him and Raja Bhalindra Singh. Then, to my surprise, he began talking to me about the future plan of Indian hockey. He talked about those who were going to be there or discarded for the next camp. I asked Mr. Ashwani Kumar in 1998 at his residence in Friends Colony why he had chosen me for the discussion about the future of Indian hockey during the finals of the 1968 Olympics in Mexico when he could have summoned any of the senior players. He solemnly replied, 'I wanted to groom you as the next Captain as you had all the credentials for captaincy and for leading the national team. Had it not been for your knee injury, your playing career would not have been cut short at a very young age, and you would have done wonders for India, and the history of Indian Hockey would have been different.'

A couple of times, Mr Ashwani Kumar had mentioned in public that the country hardly gets a half back of Balbir's calibre in a century or so. But unfortunately, it was not meant to be, so other players got the benefit owing to my knee injury.

Mourning at Sansarpur After the Mexico defeat

It was exactly 55 years ago, at the 1968 Mexico Olympics, that the men's hockey team failed to reach the Olympic final for the first time since 1928. India eventually won the bronze medal, but the defeat in the semi-final plunged all of the Sansarpur into mourning. The famous five of the squad—Colonel Balbir, Balbir (Punjab Police), Jagjit, Ajitpal and Tarsem—who hailed from the same village and brought bronze medals along with them, were afraid to set foot in it. Such deep was the village's attachment to hockey and the Indian team's fortunes that they feared the backlash.

Finishing third in the Olympics was a great shock for us; after returning to India, we were afraid to return to the village. When we finally did go home, even our parents were furious. They asked us if that was how we had learnt to play hockey. Further decades later, who would have thought that things would come to such a pass that even India's shocking incapability to reach the finals would elicit such indifference in the very village. Now, the scene is different.

Winning is Everything

The defeat at the Mexico Olympics was a deep scar. This is an entry for those who would like to understand this intense emotion involved with the game of hockey. This poem was composed by David Horsburgh for the *Illustrated Weekly of India magazine* (November 1968):

The Indian Olympic Hockey Team Returns from Mexico with Bronze Medal The Home Coming (Palam Airport Oct 1968)

No one
To meet them at the airport
Prithipal and his boys.
No joys
In the plane that brought them back.
The crime? They lost.
Do we deny
Our beaten warriors
In the dark night
Before the cock crows thrice?
Do parents spurn
Their wounded sons
Home from the battlefield?

Even cowards
Are family forgiven
These
No cowards, bravely fought
And bravely lost.

Do you know what it's like
To lose?
Your job; your wife; your son;
Your sanity or heart?
Losing is
Harder than loving
Kali entered the dice?
Do we curse Nala?
No, rather follow him with love
Through the deep forest, naked.
The difference
Between right and wrong
Gold and bronze
Success and crime
So slight; we blunder every day
Ourselves.
Spare them a thought
Sometimes

PASSING OUT PARADE AT IMA, 19 DEC 1970, RARE SIGHT OF TWO HOCKEY OLYMPIANS IN ONE FRAME. MAJ HARIPAL KAUSHIK, VrC, ON THE HORSE BACK, GC BALBIR SINGH SEEN EXTREME RIGHT, (BOTH SIKH REGT NEVER HAPPENED IN THE HISTORY OF IMA POP SO FAR.

A rare photograph of our (46 Regular) passing out parade on 19 December 1970... a matter of pride for all of us

Five Star Olympic Rings Car

I purchased my first car Premier Padmini in 1976. Only four cars used to come from Bombay in a month. Then, being an Olympian I put the five Olympic rings on the bumper and the bonnet had two hockey sticks and ball like Mercedes logo. Once, driving on the Mall Road in Jalandhar Cantonment, the Olympic rings were noticed by Lieutenant General RD. Hira, GOC, 11 Corps, who later on checked up about the owner of the car. I was summoned and asked who had authorised to put the five rings. I replied that, being an Olympian I had put them but would remove them if he so desired. Being a good sportsman, he said I could keep them so long no one objected.

He laughed that he had three stars and I had five. As long as I had possession of the car, I kept it and it was called a five-star car because the rings shone brightly. No one has had it since then.

CHAPTER 5

The Final Bow

Bombay Gold Cup April 1971

I was selected to lead the Services team for the Bombay Gold Cup at the BHA Stadium Churchgate in April 1971 and for the National Hockey Championship to be held at Bangalore in May 1971. In the semi-final of the Bombay Gold Cup versus Sikh Union, Kenya, the Kenyan team was almost like the star-studded international African team. Now, even with a niggling injury, I was in the form of my life.

As the *Times of India* dated 10 April 1971 reported: 'Services beat the Sikh Union, which had almost all the players from the Kenya National side, by one goal to nil. The Services attack was constantly on the move. It was because of the fine support they got from their intermediate line where right-half and Captain Balbir Singh not only kept a vigilant eye on the Sikh Union left wing but also moved up-field and invariably parted with the ball to an unmarked colleague, using the scoop to advantage. Balbir initiated the first danger to the Sikh Union goal when his scoop sent Ganesh tearing down the right wing. The outside right made a glorious centre, but Kenyan international fullback Avtar Singh raced back and cleared. (Tari, who hails from a Virk village in Phagwara, has led Kenya in three successive Olympics). After goalkeeper Amarjit had made a fine save of a penalty corner hit by Raminder, right-half Balbir produced another defence-splitting pass. His 40-yard scoop was picked up by Ganesh, who moved past two defenders only to be baulked by goalkeeper Amarjit in the 24th minute.' Sadly, it was at the beginning of my end.

Services Vs. Mohun Bagan Gold Cup Finals

Our opponents in the double-leg finals were mighty Mohun Bagan. We were on a roll, but there was personal danger lurking in the distance. As the local English newspaper reported: 'Some clever moves, some lucky saves, three goals and a last-minute rally, all made the first leg final of the 1971 Bombay at the BHA Stadium between Services and Mohun Bagan Calcutta, an enjoyable one. At the end of it, Services was a goal up against Mohan Bagan (Calcutta), winning the keenly- contested duel by two goals to one. The Services go into the second leg on Sunday with a one-goal advantage, and they will need it, for ten minutes before the final whistle, they lost the Services wing-half and Captain, Balbir, who wrenched a heavily bandaged knee in a fall after tackling a Bagan player. Balbir's constant prompting for Sood and Chimni, with an occasional pass to right winger Ganesh, provided the base on which Services built up sustained pressure against the Bagan goal and some of the best-combined moves of the match came from this quarter.'

We duly beat Mohun Bagan in the double leg final with a 3-1 aggregate and won the handsome trophy, but unfortunately for me and the team, in the first leg, ten minutes before the final whistle, as reported earlier, I wrenched my left knee (which had already been operated upon once) in a fall after tackling a Bagan player. Later on, the X-rays revealed a rupture of my outer ligament.

National Hockey Championship, Bangalore, 1971

After winning the Bombay Gold Cup, we moved to Bangalore as the favourite for the Rangaswamy Cup. Despite my knee injury, I played the entire tournament. I was again declared the best half-back of the Nationals. Pool B match at the Football Stadium on 28 April against the short and fighting Assamese, The Services packed just too much artillery, and we won 7-1.

In the next pool match against Bhopal, *The Sunday Statesman* headline said it all: 'Olympian Balbir sees Services through', with me having the distinction of netting the all-important goal of the match in the fifth minute. *The Deccan Herald* report by Leslie F Wilson waxed more eloquent on the subject and was headlined 'Services keep unbeaten record with Balbir's Great Goal: Services can thank their lucky stars that they had in their ranks the former Olympian and skipper, Balbir Singh who played at right-half, for it was this defender who kept his side's slate unblemished when getting the only goal against valiant Bhopal in their pool 'B' match. The only bright spot in the Services victory was Balbir's goal. A penalty-stroke specialist, Balbir's goal was a gem of the first water-undoubtedly the best seen in this league series so far. The Services skipper scooped beautifully, the ball soaring to the roof of the net, leaving goalkeeper Qamar Ali planted.'

Lathi Charged! Services Vs. Punjab Semi-Final

What transpired in the semi-final of the National Championships between Services and Punjab on Wednesday, 12 May 1971, will go down as one of my most distressing days on the field. Not because we were held goalless in the first leg semi-final and then lost the second leg, but because of a series of incidents that reduced the game to a brawl and turned hockey sticks into lathis. Strange as it may seem, the men from the cradle of hockey in our country, Punjab, played the game in the unseemliest manner. The playing arena turned into a battlefield, and, as observers mentioned later, there was only one team that tried to play in the spirit of the game. With sticks flying left, right and centre and the referee a silent spectator, it almost seemed as if our opponents had the license to hit that day. What was most shocking was that experienced Olympians like Harmik Singh, Tarsem Singh and Ajitpal Singh also adopted this style of play, trying to disrupt our game. As senior journalists reported the following day, the match was a lathi charge and carnage—a far cry from the beautiful game image that we had preserved for our national sport. As the *Deccan Herald* reported:

'Many have often wondered why India has dropped from the Olympic gold medal to the silver and finally to the bronze. Well, had you been present at the Bangalore football stadium, you would have stopped wondering. It was not hockey that was played. It was a display of arrogant rough play by men of the BSF (Border County Force) and Punjab Police who were representing Punjab against the disciplined Services team. The services, led by that fine right half and true sportsman Balbir Singh, tried to play hockey, which would have entertained the big gathering of hockey enthusiasts, but the Punjab boys would not allow them to do so, and this first leg wound up goalless.'

In the second semifinal, we lost in a tiebreaker to Punjab. We were disappointed in losing, being the better side, but we were not disgraced.

The 1971 World Cup

The IHF called 25 players for the camp of the inaugural World Cup at Barcelona in September 1971. Prior to the World Cup, the

IHF had planned to send the team to Singapore a month before. I was selected for the camp on merit, but the IHF laid down the provision that, while my leadership of the Services team and my fine display were appreciated, my final selection would depend on my physical fitness. since I was still nursing the knee injury.

After the Nationals were over, having watched all the matches, Leslie F Wilson wrote in his column in the *Deccan Herald* called 'Straight from the Shoulder' forecasting his list of 16 players most likely to be selected for the World Cup. To my surprise, he had chosen me as the captain of the team. Again, surprisingly, the IHF decided to announce the captain of the team even before the selection of the team for the Singapore tour in the executive meeting to be held in New Delhi on 11 July. This was unprecedented in the history of Indian hockey. *The Statesman*, New Delhi, too got into the prediction game and published a report datelined Chandigarh in its Friday, 9 July 1971 edition, under the headline 'Balbir or Ajitpal to Lead Team to Singapore: According to sources at the IHF, the mantle of the Captaincy of the Indian hockey team to visit Singapore on 15 August is likely to fall either on Balbir Singh of Services or Ajitpal of Punjab, both from Sansarpur. The decision will be taken on 11 July when the Executive Committee of the Federation meets in New Delhi.'

I was in Jalandhar on 9 July when I read in *The Statesman* and *The Tribune* about my being in the running for the captaincy of the forthcoming tour and World Cup. I went to the nearby Military Hospital (MH) in Jalandhar Cantonment for a medical physical fitness test. The orthopaedic surgeon at the MH, after thoroughly examining my knee, gave me a clean chit by way of a physical fitness certificate—a supreme commendation, coming as it did from no less an authority than the Army Medical Service. I didn't have so much as a cold to downgrade my Physical Category rating (crucial for active service and promotion) on the flimsiest of grounds.

Certificate in hand, I presented myself on 10 July 1971 to the IHF Chief, Ashwini Kumar, who was slated to leave for New Delhi that evening to attend the IHF executive meeting where the name of the captain of the team was to be announced. I reached Ashwini Kumar's office right on the dot at the appointed time. Showing him the Physical Fitness Certificate from the MH, I conveyed to him that I was 100% fit and had the credentials to lead the National team as the captain, provided he considered me. The conversation that took place between me and the IHF Chief is still etched sharply in my mind. He asked me whether I would accept Balbir of Railways in my team if I was made the captain (Balbir, despite his best skills as a right winger in the world, had a series of disciplinary problems, the biggest was celebrating with Pakistani players after their 1968 Olympic Gold medal win at Mexico). I replied that in case the honour was bestowed on me, I would most certainly like to have the Railwayman in my team since he was the best forward in the world, besides which I had the credentials to draw the best out of him for the sake of the Team and the Nation.

The next evening, the executive meeting decided that Ajitpal would lead the team to Singapore. It appears that intentional disinformation about my knee injury by sundry motivated individuals tilted the balance in favour of Ajitpal's selection as captain. The media reaction was expectedly furious at this strange turn of events and grave injustice.

A hard-hitting piece by R Sriman entitled 'A function Usurped' in the *Times of India,* New Delhi, on 18 July 1971 stated: 'The Indian Hockey Federation has turned in many breathtaking acts in the past, but their latest, the appointment of Ajitpal as captain for the Singapore tour should surely take the cake. The manner of his elevation to this position of honour does not exactly rebound to the credit of a premier sports organisation. Mind you, Ajitpal has not been named captain by the Selection

Committee; he has been chosen by the Executive Board of IHF! It is doubtful if a similar thing has happened anywhere else in the world. Now, the selectors are to meet at Patiala next week to choose the team. Why is it that the Executive Board has taken upon itself the function of choosing the captain in advance, thus usurping the legitimate function of the Selection Committee? It is significant that when the Selection Committee had its last full-fledged meeting at Patiala early this year in January 1971, it was Balbir Singh of Services who was chosen to lead India for the World Cup, which was to be held at Lahore in February 1971. It is not known why the claim of the Services wing half, which was good enough to merit the big honour only six months ago, has been ignored. In principle, the choice of the new captain, even assuming Balbir's fitness is open to question, should have been left to the Selection Committee, especially as they are meeting to choose the team itself.'

Team at Tikamgarh (MP), Near Jhansi, on 16 December 1971

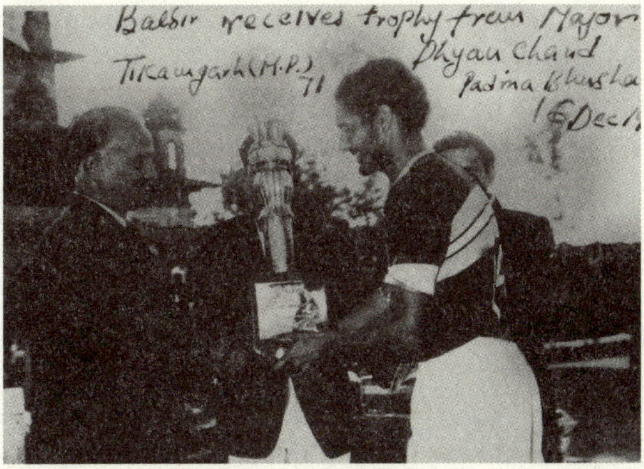

Receiving the Championship Trophy from WIZARD Dhyan Chand at Tikamgarh (MP), near Jhansi, on 16 December 1971

It is very significant that 16 December 1971 is being celebrated as Vijay Diwas by the Indian Army every year as the cease-fire was declared after the fall of Dacca and victory over Pakistan.It was amazing that three army teams participated in the Tikamgarh hockey tournament; it is rare to see that even during the war, the Army continued to pursue sports activities.

Dinner with Major Dhyan Chand at Sansarpur

Way back in 1972, the National Hockey Championship was held at Jalandhar in March-April of 1972, and Dhyan Chand was one of the National Selectors. On his request, I also invited some of the veteran hockey players from Sansarpur who had played with him in the Native Hockey Tournament in the 1930s.

I will never forget the discussion on hockey which took place that balmy evening. Everyone knew each other intimately. My father and the other four players from our village were part of the 5/13 Frontier Force Regiment that had beaten Dhyan Chand's Punjab Regiment team twice in the final of each encounter.

During the discussion, the gallant and noble soul that he was, Dhyan Chand, made it a point to repeatedly bring up that game, showering praises on the play of the 5/13 FF team, especially that of Sardar Mohan Singh. At least twice, he was heard insisting that 'Mohni' (as he called him affectionately) played better than him.

It is hardly surprising, therefore, that he was the role model for many great Olympians all over the world.

37th National Hockey Championship at Jalandhar March–April 1972

Immediately after the hockey Test match in Delhi on 7th March, all the players moved to Jalandhar to join their respective teams for their participation in the National Hockey Championship.

The *Indian Express,* on 27 March 1972, in the column by Ron Hendricks, featured: 'Services Vs. Tamil Nadu—Services beat Tamil Nadu by a one-goal margin. The Services strength in both attack and defence lay on the right flank Balbir, looked very fit.... He did a lot of covering for the centre-half Mustafa and used the ball intelligently for the Services to mount swift counterattacks.'

The *Times of India* on 7 April 1972 carried the story byLeyland de Souza: 'Semi-finals—Services Vs. Railways—The tiebreaker again. The tiebreaker was necessary to decide who should join Punjab in the final. It was Railways who made their entry, but for the 66th minute of this dour encounter, it did seem that the Services, who took the lead in the 18th minute through right-half Balbir, would make that goal count. The Services took the lead through Balbir, who, with his characteristic powerful scoop, sent the ball home against a defence that was thrown completely off balance.'

Despite displaying the best performance in the National Hockey Championship of 1972 at Jalandhar and also scoring a number of goals from the half-back position, I was not considered for the coaching camp for the Munich Olympics 1972 to be held at Lucknow because of my knee injury. In fact, I had torn a ligament of my left knee, which had already been operated upon by the famous Dr Karam Singh Grewal at Amritsar in 1969. But I was very confident that I could have played much better than Krishnamurthy, my successor, at a right-half position despite my knee injury. Since I was not called for the camp, I again decided to go for another operation and got myself admitted to the Army Hospital at Delhi Cantonment. Accordingly, I was operated upon on 18th December 1972 by a team of doctors headed by Lieutenant General AK Barat MVC, PVSM.

Beera Finally Bids Adieu to India Colours: India Vs. West Germany 7 March 1972

Despite tearing a ligament in my knee. I gave what many said was an impressive display during the two-day trials at Shivaji Stadium on 4–5 March 1972. I found I'd been selected to play the lone Test match against West Germany on 7 March 1972. We came up with a rather tepid performance against the Germans who, super-fit and hungry for victory, beat us 1-0. The lacklustre performance of the entire Indian team was a sore disappointment to the nation.

Babir seen talking to Michael Krause who scored the goal against Pakistan in 1972 Olympics on his left Carsten Keller (Capt) and on his right Wichael Peter

It was obvious that, to the Germans, the tour was an important stage in their phased assault (no doubt planned with deadly Teutonic precision and iron discipline) on the hockey gold medal at the Munich Olympics. Indeed, they carried all before them at the Munich Games (which were so tragically marred by the slaughter of the Israeli weightlifting team by Palestinian terrorists), dismantling Pakistan in a controversial final. Life often has a way of coming full circle.

Looking back at the long trail stretching behind me. I can see all the twists and turns and how all the pieces fall neatly into place. I played my first Test match against East Germany on 5 May 1966 in Jena, and ironically, the Test against West Germany at home was to be my last international match. Thanks to the defeat in the match and my earlier knee injury I was not selected to play for India in the 1972 Olympics.

It was ironic that the trail ended on my favourite ground, Lady Hardinge Stadium, now known as Shivaji Stadium. I also played the last domestic match of my career here on 30 November 1978, which I shall come to later.As National Men's Coach

As National Men's Coach

At 34, I found myself coaching the very players with whom I had shared a dressing room till a couple of years ago. I felt perfectly at ease jogging, sprinting, and stretching with them; they were, after all, my junior teammates. Thus, it fell to my lot to share with the Indian team the joys and travails of an Indian side still giddy from the euphoria of the 1980 Moscow Olympics hockey Gold medal. But two years hence, this very team was drawn to face the fierce Pakistan line-up in a televised national and international hook-up in front of a world that loves both triumphs and debacles.

Back in the old days, the coach was a friend, motivator, media manager, physio, technical advisor, strategist and sometimes even the cook, just like Shahrukh Khan's character in *Chak de India*! By some weird happenstance, I was the chief coach of the 1982 Asian Games final match. The goalkeeper for the final match, Mir Ranjan Negi, knew he would have to bear the opprobrium of being dubbed the chief architect of the greatest shame Indian hockey had ever endured in case of a loss to Pakistan in the finals, in front of a packed National Stadium!

Let us turn the clock back to six months before the Asian Games: I was informed by IM Mahajan, the then president of Indian hockey, that I was to be groomed as the future coach of Indian hockey. My big test lay just ahead... the 1982 Asian Games.

Because of the mass hysteria displayed by crazed hockey fans, it was accepted practice to stage India vs Pakistan matches at neutral venues. The Gulf was perfect for such matches: The packed (football) stadiums in Jeddah, Oman and Dubai proved to be ideal venues for these encounters, and no one could be faulted for not resenting the overwhelming hospitality. In May 1982, just six months away from Asian Games, we met the brilliant and dangerous Pakistan team at a neutral venue—the Al Nasr Stadium in Dubai—for the first-ever India-Pakistan match played under floodlights, that too on Astroturf. It was our first sight of turf since it was introduced in the 1976 Montreal Olympics

My first outing was to be a sort of baptism of fire, for I was to coach the Indian side against arch-rivals Pakistan, a side fully capable of shredding any team it faced. Unsurprisingly, we simply could not withstand the blitzkrieg of their attacking line of Kalimullah, Manzoor Jr, Hasan Sardar, Hanif, and Samiullah, with no shame in admitting that we went down fighting 0-2.

We swallowed the bitter pill knowing it was the only way of finding chinks in the Pakistan armour, a crucial requirement now that we were to try out a new combination in the final showdown in Delhi. All the while, however, we were uncomfortably aware that, to the rest of the hockey-playing world, the outcome of the final was a foregone conclusion.

In one match of the same fateful series, goalkeeper Mandapakka from Bengal Tea estates of East India failed to take decisive action at the precise moment when Hassan

Sardar was pushing the ball into the net. It was well within his reach, but he watched in a trance as the ball rolled slowly to its mark. Understandably upset, his Indian teammates rushed to berate him for his inexplicable somnolence at such a critical moment.

I, too, was puzzled how a goalkeeper, whose job was akin to that of a performing flea when it came to pulling off goalmouth saves, could stand rooted to the spot at such a crucial time. I had never seen anything like it before. It was only much later that some team members let the cat out of the bag—the goalkeeper wore contact lenses and (on account of some obscure optical aberration) couldn't see anything at certain angles! He never played for India again. The hunt for a replacement turned up Romeo James and Mir Ranjan Negi, both of whom soon found themselves clad in the team colours.

The Champions Trophy, 1982, was our best outing and Pakistan stood checkmated! Since I enjoyed the confidence of the team management and officials, I continued as the coach. It was part of my job to 'read' the games of rival players, especially the Pakistanis. and then work out various strategies to 'hold' them if one didn't want to get trampled by them, that is! The Champions Trophy in Amsterdam in June 1982 proved to be Pakistan's Waterloo: in a nail-biting match, India defeated them 5-4. Spectators, players, and sports journalists all over the world voted this match as the 'Match of the Century'—a see-saw battle to the finish! While Holland ultimately emerged the winner, we also notched up a victory of sorts almost two decades later when Indian officials signed on Australian hockey legend Rick Charlesworth's teammate Michael Nobbs to coach the Indian team. India bagged their first-ever Champions Trophy bronze medal.

After we returned, we took a short break before plunging into a lengthy training camp in the run-up to the Games.

Deshmuthu from the 1952 Olympics was the goal-keeping coach, 1972 Olympic medalist and legendary Adivasi player Michael Kindo was training the full-backs, and we all three joined our senior partner Balbir Sr. in competing for the coveted job of chief coach. Later, I got the nod as the Chief Coach and Balbir Sr. was appointed Team Manager, but confusion reigned supreme owing to our nearly identical names! We managed to put everyone in a fix, with our separate identities being established only by prefixes and suffixes!

However, had we but known it, bigger confusions lay ahead, especially that involving the selection of the team. In the movies, greying heroes gracefully adjust to playing supporting or 'character' roles. Short-distance sprinters (100m and 200m) graduate to long sprints like the 400m and 800m. In cricket, they forego T20 and one-day matches for test cricket. However, in hockey and soccer, a vastly experienced (and still valuable) player is moved back from the forward line and takes over the mantle of 'Playmaker'. It came as no surprise that Surinder Singh Sodhi, the successful skipper from the Champions Trophy was on the radar of officials. He still played a superb game and performed very well as a full-back in the inter-zonal after his Champions Trophy triumph. Nothing prepared us for what was to follow.

The IHF President and the six-member Selection Committee didn't just drop a bombshell: they dropped a star player! One fine morning, newspapers screamed that Surinder Singh Sodhi, captain of the national team, was going to be axed. The hockey fraternity was sad to hear this news. Sodhi, a sportsman first and foremost, was neither syncopated nor addlepated. He was one of those strong, silent types one reads about in PG Wodehouse novels, and his dignified, reserved nature had obviously come in the way of his bringing an apple every day for the teacher!

Unfortunately, his exclusion was carefully engineered for the express purpose of including Rajinder Sr. in the deep defence. He was a devastating penalty corner specialist, but a niggling injury had kept him away from the game for a bit too long, and his game was as rusty as his problem knee was untrustworthy.

A few days later, the next time bomb was found to be ticking. Balbir and IM Mahajan shared a mutual two-decade-old dislike for each other. It had been simmering all this time like a dormant volcano waiting to erupt. There was an ugly altercation, in the presence of probables, officials and some media persons, between the Mahajan and the legendary three-time Olympic gold medalist Balbir Singh Sr. who had just been appointed as Team Manager for the Asian Games 1982. This was just after the concluding of the trial sessions at the National Stadium had ended. After the tiff, an upset Balbir Singh Sr decided to quit the camp.

The news of the spat spread like wildfire, and Buta Singh, a political heavyweight, and the chairman of the SOC,

Captain Balbir, National Coach, motivates the team to maintain its high morale (owing to the fiery Balbir Singh (Sr) and IM Mahajan feud) National Stadium, New Delhi 24 October 1982

intervened. Eventually, Balbir Sr agreed to stay put for the sake of the country, but the damage had already been done, and the morale of the team was in tatters.

On the day of the final, the question uppermost in people's minds was—would the two Balbirs take India to the Asian Games Gold? Alas, India lost to Pakistan, and something died that day—Indian hockey. The era of India being the undisputed champion of men's hockey had ended.

National Women's Coach

I was a bit reluctant in the beginning to take over the team but later on, I was satisfied as the girls were more dedicated, punctual and disciplined than the boys. I accepted the challenge when things were not moving in the right direction. With most of the senior players having retired, I had to start from scratch, which was a very tough task ahead of me.

Record-breaking Spree of 41 Matches

Not only can Indian women become world champions they can beat world champions as well. The record winning spree of 41 matches in a row by the World Cup Olympic Champions Australia was brought to an abrupt halt.

...sure after the Asian Games, and the tournament ensured good match-practice. For a team which is in the rebuilding process, the tournament ... for Balbir Singh, who has just taken over as the National coach, it was an opportunity to see the players in action.

The victorious India Blue.

As a jubilant Indian coach, I termed the win as a superlative effort, equalling the gold India won at the 1982 Asiad in New Delhi. I had said that we would create a few surprises, and it happened. I also pointed out that striker Nidhi Khullar's and

Col Balbir Quits In Disgust

By SUNDEEP MISRA

Col Balbir, women's national hockey coach, has finally made his peace.

Fed up with his constant ongoing bickering with the Indian Women's Hockey Federation (IWHF) on the payment issue to the Indian players, Balbir Singh has put in his papers and resigned as national coach. Balbir Singh's resignation comes after a month of the World Cup finishing in Utrecht. The Indian women were placed 12th in Utrecht.

"I had already made up my mind even before the World Cup had started," Col Balbir said. "There was really no point in continuing if for every small thing you have to fight with the federation."

Balbir was rather emotional and people who knew him also know the commitment that he had for the sport. It was under his coaching that the team qualified for the World Cup, which in itself was a big achievement.

Though he wanted to quit after the World Cup, the decision was hastened by what he terms as the 'payments' issue. "Every team gets a food allowance and sometimes money just gets saved over," explained Balbir. "And whenever the team went abroad, I used to distribute this left-over allowance to the players. The federation never liked this since they wanted the money for themselves. So I had this constant argument that what is meant for the players should go the players.

"After we qualified for the World Cup in Harare, I gave the team around Rs 9,000 each when they landed in Delhi which was anyway their food allowance money but the federation president Mrs Amrit Bose didn't like it. These players don't even get a daily allowance and if they get some money out of the food allowance, it's just a small incentive for them.

"That's one reason they wanted me out because I was not fitting into their scheme of things. I saw through that and I decided to put in my papers."

Balbir was sad that he has had to walk out in this manner. "I have enjoyed working with the team and I think irrespective of them coming last in the World Cup, it's a team with lots of talent and promise. I hope

Helen Mary's game was outstanding. It was a tough tournament and good preparation for the World Cup qualifier (which was to be held in Zimbabwe in 1997). At a time when the outlook for the Indian men's hockey team was bleak, this victory was the sign of a new dawn for the women's game even if one swallow never made a summer.

The Magic Name of Balbir

There have been so many Balbirs that you can make a song about them. The Balbirs of Indian hockey confused not only opponents on the field but lovers of the game at home as well. A team with identical names, especially when they played abroad posed problems for all, including the scribes.

The name Balbir has a glorious record in Indian Hockey. It finds a mention in five Olympic and Asian games. In total they have bagged 13 medals in the Olympic Games; Balbirs have won four gold and three bronze medals and in the Asian Games they pocketed four gold and two silver medals.

L to R: Balbir Singh Kular (Pb), Balbir Singh (Sr), Dosanjh (Padmashree) Col Balbir Singh Kular (Ser) (Arjun Awardee), Balbir Singh Grewal (Rly)

Confusion of Identical Names

When William Shakespeare asked what's in a name, I am sure he didn't have the vagaries of namesakes on his mind. I have a fairly common name and have, therefore, often landed in ticklish situations.

When Balbir of the Punjab Police passed away in February 2020, some of the army officers had written a very well-worded obituary. Then I had to clarify that I am alive and kicking. Even when Balbir senior passed away in 2020, my son, Colonel Sarfraz Singh, got a few calls from serving and retired army officers expressing condolences.

So many Singhs— it's confusing!

MEXICO, Oct. 21.

MEXICAN spectators and foreign newsmen are beginning to think that India must be populated almost entirely by turbaned gentlemen surnamed Singh.

There are 13 Singhs out of 18 registered players in India's field hockey team. If one of them scores a goal—and they score plenty because India has been field hockey Olympic champion every time except once since 1928—was it scored by Ajitpal Singh or Dharam Singh or Gurbaksh or Gurbux Singh?

Or perhaps Harbinder or Harmik Singh? Of course it could always be Inder, Jagjit, Prithipal or Tarsem Singh.

If it was [illegible], however, the trouble really is at the Malaysian team.

Go to the Olympic athletics stadium and you find Bhim Singh in the men's high jump, Labh Singh in the long jump and triple jump.

Shooting singhs

In the wrestling arena, you have to distinguish between Bishamber Singh the bantamweight and Mukhtiar Singh, the welterweight.

And then of course, there are the shooting Singhs, two of whom competed in the Olympic trap event.

Karni Singh, from Bikanir, finished 10th. Randhir Singh, a 22-year-old farmer and landlord from Punjab, was 17th.

The event was won by John Braithwaite of Great Britain and neither Singh got on the victor's podium.

The medals were presented, however, by India's members of the Olympic International Shooting Committee.

Who?

Who else, but the Rajah Bhalindra Singh?—AP.

CHAPTER 6

Honours and Vignettes

Arjuna Award, 1968

The Government of India introduced the Arjuna Awards in 1961 as a means of giving recognition to outstanding sportspersons of the country. In those days, the award included a bronze statuette of Arjuna (the famed archer of the Mahabharata) and a scroll, but no cash reward. Several hockey players received this prestigious award over the years, and my turn came in the year 1968. I will not deny that this official recognition of my services to Indian hockey was extremely satisfying. The fact that I was the first hockey player to receive the award in a Gentlemen Cadet's uniform of the Indian Military Academy made it even more special for my peers as well as myself. The film division of India used to produce weekly special newsreels to highlight important events in the country in those days. The Arjuna Awards ceremony was depicted several times before the film started in the IMA cinema hall and would get standing ovations when all Gentlemen Cadets would see it before the film. It was a great honour for me. The importance of wearing my Army uniform at the Arjuna Award Ceremony at Ashoka Hall in Rashtrapati

Bhawan on 9 December 1969 has stayed with me as I was also the first Arjuna Awardee from the Sikh Regiment across all sports.

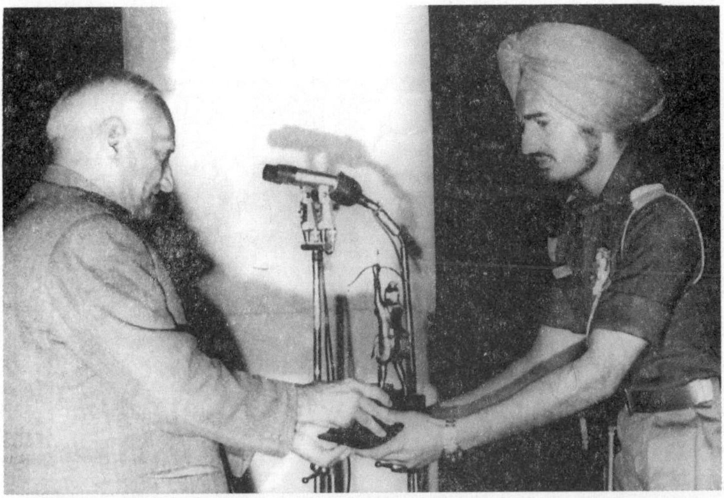

Gentleman cadet Balbir sitting between Princess Rajyashree of Bikaner and EAS Prasanna

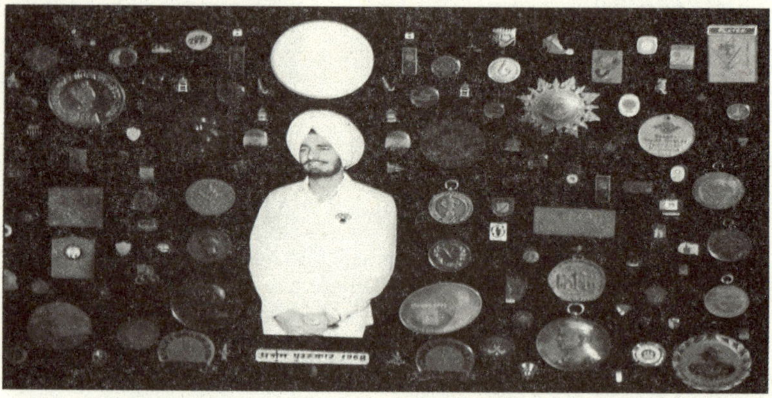

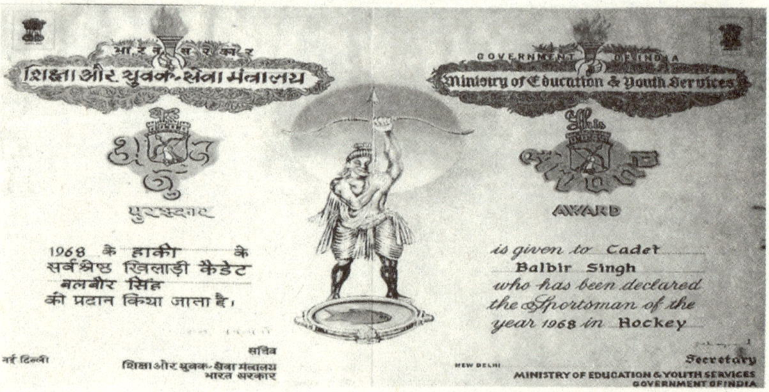

शिक्षा और युवक-सेवा मंत्रालय

पुरस्कार

1968 के हाकी के
सर्वश्रेष्ठ खिलाड़ी कैडेट
बलबीर सिंह
को प्रदान किया जाता है।

सचिव
नई दिल्ली
शिक्षा और युवक-सेवा मंत्रालय
भारत सरकार

GOVERNMENT OF INDIA
Ministry of Education & Youth Services

AWARD

is given to Cadet
Balbir Singh
who has been declared
the Sportsman of the
year 1968 in Hockey

NEW DELHI
Secretary
MINISTRY OF EDUCATION & YOUTH SERVICES
GOVERNMENT OF INDIA

Bronze Medal
Champions Trophy
1982
as a coach

Gold Medal
Asian Games
1966
as a player

Army Medal
Vishisht Seva Med
1982-84
as a soldier

"A medal is something you hang on the wall. It is an out come of journey and struggle
It's very important to focus on the journey because that is what counts.
Sports teaches you important lessons."

Balbir receives the Nehru Cup from Dr Fakurdin Ali Ahmed, the President of India

Balbir shakes hand with Dr Zail Singh, The President of India

Balbir being introduced to Dr SD Sharma, President of India, at Rashtrapati Bhavan

Balbir With Prime Minister PV Narsimha Rao at Dhyan Chand Stadium, Delhi

One act of the erudite Sardar especially impressed me; Manmohan Singh,Prime Minister of India, poured out tea for Balbir Sr and offered him the cup with his own hands, out of sheer deference to Balbir's age and seniority at the launch of his book at 7 Race course

Field Marshal K M Cariappa

Field Marshal Cariappa was a true sportsman, disciplinarian to the core, and very fearless. I met him when he was the chairman of the Sports Council of India and got the chance to travel with him on the Air India flight as a member of the Indian team for the Hamburg International in May 1966.

In May 1971, while leading the services team that played the first-ever hockey match against the Coorg XI at Marcera, I got the opportunity to visit his house in Marcera at the hilltop. In 1967, during the Services Hockey Championship at Egmore Stadium Madras, he paid a visit to witness the hockey match without informing the organisers. He sat in the spectators' wooden stand enclosure. After some time, he was spotted by Wing Commander Mall, Secretary SSCB, who requested him to sit in the VIP Box, but he did not agree and saw the full match from there—a rare thing to happen.

In Dec 2018, I went to see the World Cup hockey at Bhubaneswar, and after that, I planned to go to Bangalore, but as luck would have it, I was allotted the same guest room which was permanently earmarked for Field Marshal Cariappa whenever he would visit Bangalore and ASC Centre (South). That guest room has been named as Cariappa Guest Room.

Air Marshal Arjun Singh

In December 1964, after the final of the Services Hockey Championship at Lady Hardinge in Delhi, I had the privilege to receive the first cup from then Air Chief Arjun Singh while on the rolls of 4 SIKH. Then, I met him at the Delhi Golf Course and had the honour of having tea with him.

Field Marshal Sam Manekshaw

General Sam Manekshaw inspects the Parade at the Army Cadet College Poona in 1967--Cadet Balbir is seen in the front

Balbir receives the Vishisht Seva Medal from the Chief of the Army Staff General AS Vaidya

Walk the Talk with Mr Atal Bihari Vajpayee in Oct 1982

I had the honour of meeting nine Presidents of India and seven prime ministers of India. But I had the privilege of meeting, Mr Atal Bihari Vajpayee, while he was on his regular morning walk with two Pomeranian dogs. I spotted him near the India Gate on Rajpath and introduced myself as the National Hockey Coach. I walked along with him for four to five minutes and discussed the finer nuances of the game knowledgeably. He himself was a good hockey player in his college days.

How I missed the Brigadier's Rank

I was to retire on 30 April 1997. The selection board for my next promotion (to the rank of Brigadier) was held in January 1997, but the result was not declared till the date of my retirement. I came to know through reliable sources that I was through for my next promotion. In the Army, promotion is based on there being an available vacancy. I approached the then Minister of State for Defence, the late NV Somu, for an extension to pick up my rank. I was given a three-month extension, till 31 July 1997, vide no. 8(14)/96/D(MS) Govt. of India, Ministry of Defence New Delhi, dated 6 May 1997, which conveyed the sanction of the President, keeping in view my services to the nation, a rare occurrence in the Army. This was only the second such instance, the first being given to Major General BS Malik. However, I lost the opportunity to become a Brigadier due

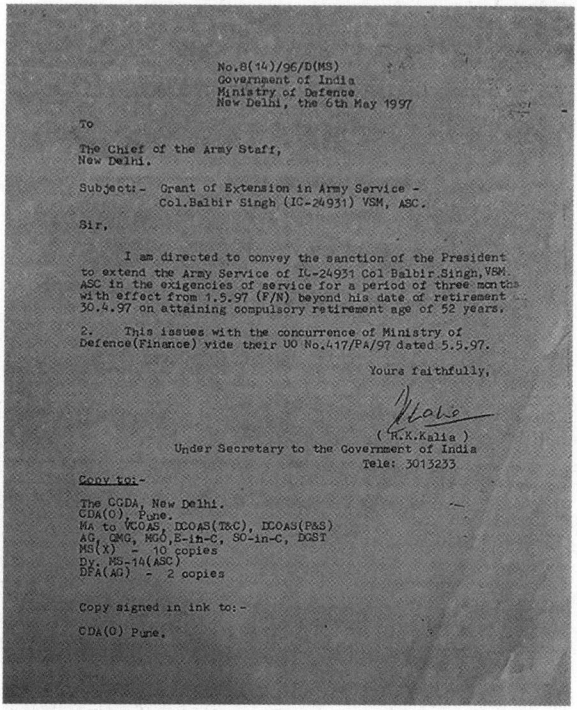

No.8(14)/96/D(MS)
Government of India
Ministry of Defence
New Delhi, the 6th May 1997

To

The Chief of the Army Staff,
New Delhi.

Subject:- Grant of Extension in Army Service -
Col.Balbir Singh (IC-24931) VSM, ASC.

Sir,

I am directed to convey the sanction of the President to extend the Army Service of IC-24931 Col Balbir Singh, VSM. ASC in the exigencies of service for a period of three months with effect from 1.5.97 (F/N) beyond his date of retirement 30.4.97 on attaining compulsory retirement age of 52 years.

2. This issues with the concurrence of Ministry of Defence(Finance) vide their UO No.417/PA/97 dated 5.5.97.

Yours faithfully,

(R.K.Kalia)
Under Secretary to the Government of India
Tele: 3013233

Copy to:-

The CGDA, New Delhi.
CDA(O), Pune.
MA to VCOAS, DCOAS(T&C), DCOAS(P&S)
AG, QMG, MGO, E-in-C, SO-in-C, DGST
MS(X) - 10 copies
Dy. MS-14(ASC)
DFA(AG) - 2 copies

Copy signed in ink to:-

CDA(O) Pune.

to my involvement with hockey. I had to go to Harare on 24 July with the women's hockey team as the chief coach for the World Cup qualifying tournament. Before I left the country, it was confirmed by the MOD that there was a provision for another extension so I could pick up the rank on my return on 14 August 1997. But when I spoke to Mr NN Vohra, then

Principal Secretary with the Prime Minister, from the residence of the High Commissioner of India in Harare on 31 July, I learnt that the Army Chief, General Shanker Ray Chowdhary, had prevailed upon the Defence Minister, Mulayam Singh Yadav, to retire me on 31 July as 'the officer was not physically present in the country', which advice the Defence Minister followed. In retrospect, I gave precedence to the national cause and so missed my promotion. The fact that the girls qualified for the World Cup made me forget my disappointment.

Balbir ta Sadda Munda Hai

Lieutenant General DS Kalha, Director of General Supply and Transport, who was also the manager of the India-bound Mexico Olympic Team in 1968, was keen that I join the Army Service Corps (ASC). However, it was difficult for him to convince Lieutenant General Harbaksh Singh of the Sikh Regiment. That nasty knee injury had denied me two Olympics and all but barred me from joining 1 SIKH or 4 SIKH as a Commissioned Officer. I later joined the ASC on the request of General Kalha as General Harbaksh relented and granted sanction for the same. However, the Sikh Regiment General used to convey to the hockey fraternity that whenever he met me in public, he would announce with pride, '*Balbir Ta Sada Munda Hai*' (Balbir is our boy).

Indeed, when British officers Major John Ennis and Captain Alan Wimbush, who had served the 36 SIKH (later 4 SIKH) during the Second World War, attended its centenary celebration in 1987 and then paid a visit to General Harbaksh and came to Shivaji Stadium to see the hockey match during the Nehru hockey tournament, he told them in Punjabi *'Balbir ta sada munda hai. Sikh paltan join nahi kar sakia kyun ke goda khrab ho gaya.'* And the British officer replied, 'You mean the knee.' All the British officers attached to the regiments spoke the language which the troops could understand. They preferred to speak to me in fluent Punjabi, and I was amazed to see how they remembered the language so well.

World's Most Feared Full Backs of the 50s and 60s

Balbir standing left, with two great full backs of 1950s and 1960s—RS Gentle, triple gold medallist in 1948, 1952 & 1956 and Prithipal, triple Olympian—1960 Silver, 1960 Gold, 1968 Bronze

Prithipal Singh

Prithpal's bone-snapping bullet-like shots made opposing players leap out of the way to save themselves, as seen in the 1964 Tokyo Olympics, where he scored 11 goals. Not only European but Pakistani players were scared of facing Prithipal when he was in the possession of the ball.

In the April 1964 Nationals at Lady Hardinge Delhi, he broke the shin bone of Major Singh of Punjab, who was defending the penalty corner against Railways, with a stinging shot. Then I saw him scoring the winning goal with a powerful shot against West Germany in the Ahmedabad International in 1961. My association began with him in the 1966 Asian Games, and then I played under his captaincy in the Madrid International 67 and Mexico Olympics 1968.

FIH brought in the stick rule due to Prithipal's style of hitting several goals, but despite that, he was the top scorer in the Mexico Olympics. I, too, scored four goals, and if the goal against the Japanese was considered, five goals then. I topped the list with more goals than Prithipal. In the 1968 Olympics, I used to stand in the goal while defending the penalty corner, which Prithipal insisted because of my perfection in stopping the ball. In the words of Munir Dar, Olympian and captain of Pakistan, 'Prithipal was the best fullback of 60's a *sherdil* player. Before the final match against Pakistan in the Asian Games in 1966, Prithipal gave a massive dose of inspiration, without sounding communal, to assert the pride of *jooris* (top knot,) hinting to the nine Sikhs players.

I feel sorry to share that despite his name and fame, he met with a tragic end.

RS Gentle

RS Gentle played in 1948, 1952 and 1956, when he was the vice-captain of the team and scored the winning goal against Pakistan from the penalty corner, the first meeting against Pakistan in the Olympics at Melbourne. India was lucky that Pakistan missed the chance to score from a penalty bully, which was taken by Amir Kumar of India and centre forward Hamidi from Pakistan. Amir Kumar cleared the ball with the back sticks, which was a legitimate goal if the defender committed the foul, but the Australian umpire gave his decision in India's favour. In December 1982, as a coach of the Indian team, I was in Melbourne for the ESANDA World Cup. I visited the same stadium in Melbourne with Balbir senior, who narrated about the victory over Pakistan, and he showed me the spot from where Randhir Singh Gentle scored the winning goal against Pakistan in the final.

I was never offered drinks until 10 November 1977 when the late RS Gentle, Olympian and my coach invited me to dinner at his residence when I happened to be in Bombay for the Guru Teg Bahadur Gold Cup. I went in his Fiat car, and he purchased a bottle of whiskey and two bottles of beer near the King Circle en route to his house, where I tasted beer for the first time in my life with my coach. Later, I took to social drinking but in a small quantity and controlled measure.

I am lucky to have associations with the two most feared fullbacks in the world.

Dinner at Balbir Senior's Christened Olympia House, Chandigarh

For the Inter-Services Championship held in Chandigarh in February 1974, we braved the cold as we travelled on a Vespa two-wheeler all the way from Jalandhar. We were treated like royalty over dinner at Balbir's house—the first dinner after our marriage. There, we had the pleasure of meeting senior Singh's wife and his three kids. Commander Nandi Singh, Olympian, and Balbir Singh Junior of Sansarpur, Asian Games player of 1958 Tokyo, were also present.

Punjab Dances to Bulbul Carapiet's tune

The British, for all their cynical colonialism, were known for vigorously popularising sports throughout the 'Empire'. Initially dazed by the heat and humidity, they rallied their energetic natures and decided to keep up the practice of their favourite games such as squash, cricket, croquet, tennis and football.

In 1927, the first Railway Athletics meet was conducted at Delhi's Central Park. The idea was to occupy idle time to channel their energies. In doing so, they demonstrated the skill, speed and strength essential ingredients in sports. It is no secret, therefore, that modern sport in India owes its origins to the British and the colonial Raj. Perhaps the most skilful Anglo-Indian to have ever played for India was Bulbul Carapiet. Of Armenian descent, born in Persia, studied in Darjeeling, worked in Calcutta, and spoke Hindi and Bengali, he showed rare discrimination by swearing only in rustic Punjabi. This, and the fact that he was the first southpaw in the world of Hockey, made him stand out from the crowd.

My earliest memory of Bulbul, an amazingly fine-looking man, goes back to the quarter-final between Punjab and West Bengal in the 1956 Rangaswamy Cup. The host (Punjab) lost to West Bengal in the knock-out quarter-final stage of the tournament, thanks to an excellent goal scored by inside left Carapiet. This means I have enjoyed the privilege of seeing Maradona's brand of sorcery in hockey! And that, too, decades before Diego Armando Maradona became a household name. If anyone wants an example of Back to the Future, this was it. Carapiet received the ball near the half line. He mesmerised the future India skipper Charanjit Singh (1964 Olympic skipper) and tall and handsome Gurjit Singh (1958 Asian Games Silver medallist) in the Punjab half and he hoodwinked the Olympian right back Bakshish Singh. As he approached Raj Kumar, the Punjab goalkeeper, his feint deceived the goalkeeper so much that Raj Kumar lost his balance and fell. Carapiet saw the goalie flat on the ground before the yawning goalmouth. With the icy precision of a professional assassin, he gently pulled the ball back with the tip of his stick and delicately tapped it into the unguarded goal on the other side of the helpless custodian. If it hadn't happened on the hockey field, it would have qualified for the ultimate crime—a cold-blooded murder! If I'd worn a hat, I'd have doffed it in sheer admiration for this iconic 'lefty'. Never had I seen such a goal, and never again (with one or two notable exceptions) did I see such a classic bamboozling of the goalie, followed by the perfect coup de grace. In his mid-80s and almost blind due to diabetes, Bulbul vividly remembers the move but, sadly enough, has forgotten his Punjabi skills.

Sitting in my favourite rocking armchair and sipping my favourite whiskey, my mind often wanders back to thoughts of hockey past and present. At such times, I cannot help but wonder how great an icon Carapiet (who died in Australia) would have been had he played today, what with television having taken the game into every home across the globe. The visual media would have lionised Carapiet even as his stellar performances kept their cash registers ringing. A similar goal was scored by Iniesta of Spain against China. Iniesta, the fleet-footed midfielder, had the attacking flair; picking the ball up wide on the left, he surged past his marker into the area and pulled the ball back stranded goalkeeper Zeng of China, side foot into the empty net on 5 June 2012. That broke down the dogged Chinese defence.

Udham Singh: The King Without a Kingdom

Only a player of Dhyan Chand's calibre could stand the test of time. Other names are often submerged under the waves of history and do not receive the same adulation. But there are also some whose greatness, for whatever reasons, was never highlighted, so they never got the recognition they so richly deserved. In retrospect, Udham Singh of Sansarpur was just such a gem, a king without his crown. Unassuming and

Olympians from Sansarpur (L to R): Udham Singh Kular, Gurmit Singh Kular, Colonel Balbir Singh Kular and Jagjit Singh Kular

soft-spoken, he played in 1952, 1956, 1960 and 1964 Olympic medal-winning teams. His relative obscurity is mainly due to his propensity for finding ingenious ways to dodge the spotlight.

My memory of Udham derives from the same tournament. A mere nine-year-old lad, I watched in astonishment as arguably the greatest Sansarpuri took on the field, demolished the opponent's defence and bamboozled the goalkeeper by putting him on the wrong foot, finishing it off with a gentle tap. He made it look so easy and effortless. Then, in characteristic fashion, 'Udhi' as he was known in hockey circles, would quietly retreat to his own half: showmanship was alien to Udham's nature, a man who reputedly slept with his hockey stick beside his pillow. The Services team showcased some of the finest hockey skills, mixed with generous dollops of style and synchronisation—the new dynamics of the game. Unfortunately, there was no yardstick to measure who, among the contemporary stars, was the best player. But there was definite consensus among observers that even in that elite team, Udham had the credentials to be recognised as a player of towering stature. His other greatness was in the longevity of his career. Udhi was short-listed in the 1948 Indian Olympic squad and played for his department team, Punjab Police and later Border Security Force (BSF) as late as the 1980s. This was way after I retired from all forms of hockey—his mantra—a nutritious, controlled diet (sans liquor), ample sleep and regular practice. Older folks from our village had seen Udhi dribbling the ball on the Mall Road of Jalandhar cantonment. His prowess lay in trapping the ball and making it roll around the rival's defence. So fluid and guileful were his movements during his excursions that the rival defence was visibly alarmed whenever Udham got hold of the ball.

I did not realise it then, but the dimension of competitive hockey that had witnessed for the first time in my life at that tender age would serve to inspire me in myriad ways thereafter. Today, in my late seventies, I can still recollect the dazzling moves and goals of that tournament as clearly as if I'd seen them only yesterday.

Au Revoir, Ball Boy Satti

You fool, why couldn't you convert a simple pass into a goal? Even I could have done it with one touch! So thundered Satti after losing to a famous international player who had just

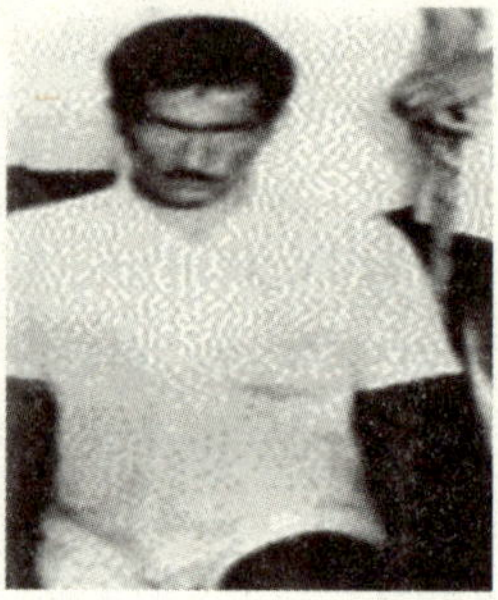

missed a sitter. This renowned player, who later played for India and even captained India briefly, was infuriated, not because his team members were relishing his discomfiture but because the admonition came from of all people, Satti, the ballboy of Delhi stadium Satti I must have been in his 30's at the time and stayed in the servant quarters at Delhi's famous Hanuman Temple in Connaught Place, near Lady Hardinge stadium. He was a ball boy during the match (a voluntary and honorary position), but he was also a friend to senior players and a guide to outstation players in Delhi as revealed in their first outing. He was such a general part of team meetings and unfailingly accompanied the boys when they were on tour. The above incident was folklore for decades... but I have another story to share. All matches played between 1965 and 1990 would have given viewers a special treat, as just before every match, Satti would circumambulate the ground three times before placing the ball with great ceremony smack in the centre of the ground. Then, he would turn around smartly and salute towards the VIP stand to thunderous applause. He was a celebrity in his own right.... a ball boy with a difference. In his colourful outfit, he would manage the entire match on his own... what zeal! He would travel to Mumbai, Hissar, Gwalior, Agra... Before a university match at Hissar was due to begin, Satti was performing his customary act when the buttons of his shorts gave way and the all-too-brief garment, helplessly obeying the force of gravity, gathered at his ankles! As poor Satti froze with embarrassment, the initially thunderstruck university boys leapt to his support, forming a human chain around him and escorting him, in all his natural finery, back to the dressing room! We laughed and laughed till the tears ran down our cheeks. His dedication to the game impressed me to the extent that I once invited him over to my army officers' mess for breakfast. I wanted to thank him personally and reward him for his contribution to the game now that my playing days were drawing to a close. A day before we were to meet, I handed him a necktie and told him to wear it on his best shirt when he came to visit me at the officers' mess at Agra. Proud as a peacock at the singular honour bestowed upon him, he turned up on the dot to keep the RV (army shorthand for rendezvous). He had worn the necktie and his best shirt, but, to my horror, he'd also worn a vastly oversized coat—one that was obviously borrowed. It was a comical sight but also a touching one. Here was a simple, great-hearted man who was reaping the rewards of a lifetime of fanatical dedication to his insignificant role in a very big game. Satti's deeds reminded me of the words of Sir Henry Royce, Founding Partner of Rolls-Royce: 'Whatsoever is rightly done, however humble, is noble.' Pride and gratitude blazed from those soft brown eyes, mirroring my respect and appreciation: What we give to others has a way of returning to us. Sadly, Satti passed away soon afterwards due to cirrhosis of the liver, his love for life and his love for the bottle had fought for supremacy, and the latter had won. A small life it was and, in the ways of men, soon forgotten, so I guess this is my feeble attempt at perpetuating his memory. Men like Satti are rare. They grow out of their traditional role and develop a knack for flamboyant showmanship, thus adding a missing dimension to humdrum human affairs. If the game was the peacock, Satti was its feathers and, in a very special way, the more lovable of the two.

He taught by example that we can choose to limit ourselves to conventional roles in life, or we can choose to grow wings and soar above the crowd of ordinary earthbound men. By his creative interpretation of his place in the greater scheme of things, he brought joy, glory and respectability to the work of a humble ball boy guess we need more such characters in Indian hockey today. Better still, perhaps some philanthropist or an altruistic organisation will institute an award named after him to keep alive his never-say-die spirit and promote all that he stood for.

Hockey Goalkeeper Havildar Kirpa Ram, VrC, 4 SIKH, Hero of the Battle of Walong, 1962

The Army has a logistic tail, which was traditionally referred to as 'Followers' in campaigns, and they were also described as tradesmen, now carry weapons and practice firing regularly. In good units, like the Saragarhi Battalion, a desire to be a part of action has always been there, even among this lot. For example, Daad, in 1897, was a sweeper by trade but an equally valiant fighter in combat. A few members of this intrepid lot also excelled in the sports arena. Havildar Kirpa Ram of 4 SIKH was an ace shooter and master at basic infantry tactics as he voluntarily took part in all training. He was a man blessed with exceptional leadership qualities, and these were particularly evident on the hockey field, whom I had seen playing as a young boy of 10 years in Jalandhar Cantonment in the Services Hockey Championship in 1956. Like on the hockey field, he took charge and fought like a man possessed during the Battle of Walong against the Chinese in 1962.

Kirpa Ram was the one who had tamed and looked after the unit mascot, Rani, a female Panther. She followed him like a lamb, and if Kirpa Ram was to be believed, he was the reason 4 SIKH got the grades it did in inspections.

He would feed meat to the cub, buying from outside when it was not available in the langar. The cub was taken by him and chained, with an iron mask on its face, whenever he went for game practice.

He belonged to Village Birring in Jalandhar Cantonment, about 3 kilometres from Sansarpur. Later, his son Ram Murthy, who joined the BSF hockey team, represented the national hockey team in 1969 at the Bombay International Hockey tournament. Kirpa Ram was known for his ready loyalty, selfless service and humour in the battalion, cheered by one and all in the regiment and as well as in the SIKH Regimental Centre. While playing the goalkeeper of the hockey team, he was called the dependable goalkeeper, being the last line of defence.

The Battle of Walong in 1962 revealed Kirpa Ram's unwavering bravery and resourcefulness. Despite being classified as a non-combatant, he willingly participated in combat operations and courageously supplied ammunition to the frontlines. When faced with a Chinese ambush, he fearlessly led his team, enduring injuries as they pushed through the enemy's grip. When the company faced heavy casualties and made the difficult decision to retreat, Kirpa Ram volunteered to stay behind with the rear party—a group predominantly composed of unit sportsmen tasked with safeguarding the withdrawal. Amid mounting pressure and dwindling ammunition, Kirpa Ram fearlessly rallied the team for a daring counterattack. Charging out of the trenches with bayonets in hand, they engaged the Chinese forces despite the overwhelming odds. Tragically, the entire rear party, including Kirpa Ram, sacrificed their lives in the fierce and heroic action. Their selfless determination paved the way for the remaining survivors of the company to escape the clutches of the enemy. The Battle of Walong left an indelible mark on 4 SIKH, with the loss of numerous sportsmen, including five national-level medallists. Amid the heartache, Kirpa Ram's gallantry shone brightly, earning him the posthumous recognition of the Vir Chakra—an esteemed honour usually reserved for combatants. His unwavering spirit and exceptional leadership continue to inspire others, leaving an enduring legacy that echoes through time. Kirpa Ram's extraordinary journey serves as a timeless reminder to all who follow in his footsteps to strive for courage, selflessness, and unwavering commitment in the face of adversity.

Invariably, the tradesmen have one request—that the letter sent to their home address should mention only their rank and not include their trades, as it is customary to write Havildar (Boot Maker), and Havildar Kirpa Ram was very particular about it, being a Services-level hockey player.

'It is foolish and wrong to mourn the men who died. Rather, we should thank God that such men lived'.

Subedar Modan Singh (aka Modi): Most Feared Full-back in Domestic Hockey (4 SIKH)

Long after our playing days are over, we hockey veterans can't help narrating anecdotes whenever we unite at any hockey tournament. Some players are remembered for their antics. The burly Modan Singh (Modi), a one-time SRC fullback, was one

such player. They say old sportsmen, like old soldiers, never die; they just fade away, exchange banter, and compare notes and tell tales.

A few years ago, I turned up at the Shivaji Stadium, KG Kakar, player, umpire, commentator, and official, joined the veteran players to add his own brand of humour by describing an incident involving full-back Modan. Once, when SRC was playing against an Indian university, a young man called Puran Singh, a very promising player of Meerut, was part of the university team. Since Modan Singh was known for his rough play, it so happened that Puran Singh could hoodwink the ferocious full-back Modan Singh in the first half, and immediately he conveyed to Puran Singh, 'Kaka don't play this type of hockey. You got a bright future to play for the country; otherwise, you will repent.' Puran did not pay much heed to this, and again, he tried to dodge Modan Singh, who swung his heavy stick on his legs. Puran Singh was seen crying on the field for help, and later, he was taken off the field on a stretcher. When Kakar warned Modan for his act, pat came the reply that he had told Puran not to dodge him and that he should have played his passes from a safe distance. His father, Harbans Singh, a former hockey player who had come from Meerut especially to see the match, hurled abuses at Modan and lamented that his son's career could have been finished.

A fierce Modan Singh was always an irksome and dangerous player as hazardous for an opponent as a minefield. He was never a welcome sight to the opposition. Modan was known for these habitual acts; he could have played for India but for his rough play. Despite hitting the opponent with his stick and sharp elbow, he used to hound and harry on a number of occasions, hold physically and tug at the opponent forwards. Many outstanding forwards of his time used to be scared of him. They would literally avoid playing against him. It is sad to note that once powerful SRC, Champions of Nehru Hockey 1965 and winners of the Dhyan Chand Hockey Tournament against a team from Pakistan in 1952 Delhi, now find it difficult even to field a team in the tournament.

Sardars of Hockey: Ten Legends

26 April 2006 saw some of the biggest names in Indian hockey getting together at Hotel Ashoka in New Delhi to select the 10 best Sikh players who had played for the country. The ten-member jury headed by the former Chief Justice JS Verma and comprising former Olympians like Leslie Claudius, Group Captain RS Bhola, Lieutenant Colonel Haripal Kaushik, former IHF President IM Mahajan and four journalists—Jaganadha Rao (former Sports Editor, PTI), S Thyagarajan (Sports Editor, The Hindu), Prabhjot Singh (Chief of Bureau, The Tribune) and Dilbahra (London District Police Chief and UK hockey official). Balbir Singh (Senior) was chosen as the best among the lot by the panel. It was a rare sight. The players who created awe in the minds of

L to R: Pargat Singh, Harbinder Singh, Col Balbir Singh, Balbir Singh (Sr) and Ajitpal Singh

their rivals on the field and for decades had lived in the hearts of their fans recounted interesting tales of those golden days now confined to history books. My elder sister, Mandish Kaur, accepted the award bestowed on the late Udham Singh of Sansarpur. She spoke on the occasion, saying, 'He (Udham) was a role model for Sansarpur hockey players; I still remember that whenever he went for practice, Balbir, Ajitpal, and Tarsem would follow him. Now that both Balbir and Ajitpal have also been picked as top players, I would like to ask them to do something for hockey.' The idea of honouring the 'Sardars of Indian Hockey' was originated by Sandeep Mishra of indianhockey.com fame and the chosen best ten were Balbir Singh (Senior), Udham Singh, Dharam Singh, Prithipal Singh, Harbinder Singh, Colonel Balbir Singh (Services), Balbir Singh (Railways), Ajitpal Singh, Surjit Singh, and Pargat Singh.

Sarfraz Meeting Bishan, Prasanna, Chandu Borde, and Gavaskar in 1985 at Wankhede Stadium, Bombay, During the Ranji Trophy Final

I had gone to Bombay from Gaya, where I was posted, to receive the Vishisht Sena Medal (VSM). My family joined me from Jalandhar.

We stayed with my brother-in-law, an Indian Navy Lt Cdr, at the Madh Island Naval base. My son Sarfraz, then in class III, insisted on meeting Sunil Gavaskar. He had recently seen Gavaskar being presented with the keys of a Maruti 800.

Since the Ranji Trophy match was in full swing, I asked K L Passi, the Secretary of the IHF and Bombay Hockey Association, to arrange passes for us.

Just as we entered the main gate, we ran into cricket legend Bishan Singh Bedi, EAS Prasanna, and Chandu Borde.

They invited us to join them for tea in their room at the Garware Club. My son kept repeating his desire to meet Gavaskar. Bedi said jokingly in Punjabi that they were no less than Gavaskar! Since the Bombay team was fielding, I had to wait till the end of the match to meet Gavaskar. Prasanna introduced Sarfraz to his hero, and it was a memorable moment for him.

In 2003, I took my son to meet Bedi, who happened to be staying at the Radisson Hotel in Jalandhar. On meeting Sarfraz, the first thing Bedi wanted to know was whether this was the same little boy who had once wanted to meet Gavaskar! What a sharp memory 'Paaji' has! Relaxed and confident, a thing Bedi wanted to know was where the great humourist and loyal friend, Bishan, is a cricketing hero in his own right - one of the greatest spinners the game has ever seen.

Bishen Singh Bedi receives the trophy at Sansarpur from Mr Umrao Singh, former Sports Minister of Punjab, with Coloner Balbir Singh, President of Sansarpur Hockey Association by his side in 2002

Bishen Singh Bedi with hockey Olympians at Sansarpur

Colonel Balbir Singh and Surinderjit

Colonel Manjot Singh (Son-in-law), Colonel Sarfraz Singh (Son), Colonel Balbir Singh, Surinderjit (Wife), Amanjot (Daughter-in-law), Kiran (Daughter)

Mrs and Col Balbir Singh on their 50th Anniversary

Major Naranjan Singh Sangha (4 BIHAR), my father-in-law, was presented a Katana (a Samurai Sword) by a Japanese Lieutenant General during a dining out party in the British Officers Mess at Changi, Singapore, five hours before the Japanese General was hanged for war crimes during WWII. As per true British traditions, the British-Indian infantry unit located near Changi prison invited three Japanese generals convicted for war crimes in full ceremonials for dining out. The sword was presented after the dining-out speech by the Japanese General to the Indian Major as he happened to be the officiating CO senior-most officer present in the mess. The priceless historic possession rests with the family of Colonel Sarfraz Singh.

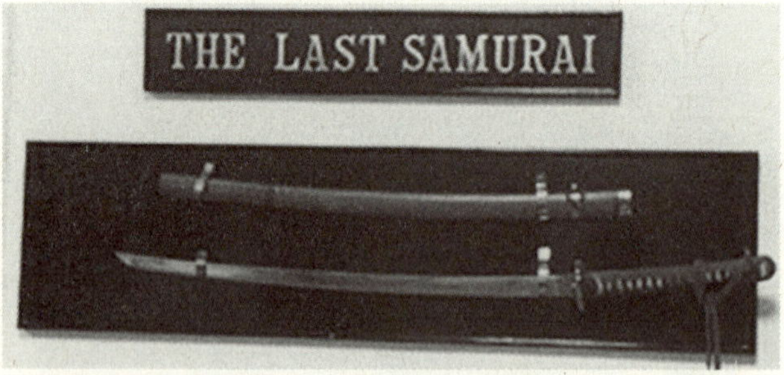